ORIGINAL INNOCENCE

The Three Mysteries of Life Revealed

WILLIAM F. FECHTER PhD

with

JOSIE VARGA

ORIGINAL INNOCENCE

WILLIAM F. FECHTER PhD

TO NICOLE
THANKS FOR
BEING SO NICE
Blessings
William Fechter PhD

CONTENTS

ACKNOWLEDGMENTS

First, I would like to acknowledge Dr. W. Edwards Deming and his understanding of the relationship of variation and quality. It was from his 1982 book entitled *Quality, Productivity, and Competitive Position*, and after eight years of teaching his examples of understanding variation, that I had a profound revelation of its relationship to the imperfections in the relative-phenomenal world. This revelation was instrumental in my discovery of the origin of ignorance.

Next, I would like to thank Dr. Thomas Hora and his books and tapes on Metapsychiatry. These books and tapes have been influential in my view of reality. His spiritual teachings have truly been a beneficial presence in my life. His definition of God as love-intelligence has been used throughout this book.

It was through Dr. Hora's book *Beyond the Dream: Awakening to Reality* that I came to know that the origin of suffering was indeed ignorance. So I asked the next logical question: what is the origin of that ignorance? I now believe that his spiritual guidance from the other side aided in my discovery of the answer to that question.

I would also like to thank Josie Varga for her belief in me as a sincere seeker into the mysteries of life. I had all but given up on this book when Josie, like an angel from New Jersey, came along and agreed to help with it. She once told me this book was the most difficult project she had ever worked on.

Besides being an author and former communications consultant, Josie also served as the director of communications and editor for a trade association. As a speaker, she helps the bereaved by sharing her message that life never ends and love never dies. She also teaches others to focus on the positive, explaining why happiness is all a matter of how we think.

Of course, it would be impossible to thank everyone, as I have studied and read hundreds of spiritual, religious, and scientific books and have experienced much joy and suffering, and many rejections, during more than two decades of being a sincere seeker into these mysteries of life. To those who have been supportive, and even to those who have rejected my views of reality, I want to say thank you all.

DEFINITIONS OF KEY WORDS

God: the Infinite Source and Ultimate Reality of all that is or ever will be

Oneness: God is All and All and within all

Creation: inherent necessity of Oneness to express its dynamic potential

Creation process: from the stillness of infinite awareness to the dynamic reality of relative-phenomenal worlds of conscious beings

Spirit: the essence of God in every soul

Love: a quality of spirit

Soul: that which is an eternal expression of God

Consciousness: a flow of thoughts with degrees of awareness

Awareness: that which is beyond the duality of consciousness

Relative: the variation in all things

Phenomena: temporal and transient appearances

Relative-phenomenal world: the variation of appearances

Infinite: that which has no boundaries

Karma: what we sow, we reap

Ego: the belief that we are a separate self from all others

Innocence: inexperience and blamelessness

Ignorance: the effect of inexperience

Heaven: the loving hereafter

Divine Intelligence: understanding the underlying reality of appearances

Intellectual aptitude: an IQ (intelligence quotient) test and rating

Expression: that which makes God a dynamic reality

Wisdom: a divine awareness that comes from life experiences

Spiritual discernment: seeking the wisdom of the spiritual realm

Sincere seeker: the path of spiritual discernment

Involution: when the oneness of God becomes many souls

Evolution: the evolution of the soul to a greater awareness of its divine self

INTRODUCTION

"Truths and roses have thorns about them."
—Henry David Thoreau

Since the dawn of mankind, humans have had a quest for knowledge and understanding. Our pursuit for knowledge has created many religious and scientific beliefs that are based on judging by appearances.

History has shown that sages, prophets, and mystics have taught their followers not to judge by appearances. The underlying reality of appearances is a human longing for meaning, purpose, joy, creativity, compassion, and unconditional love.

Every sincere seeker has looked up into the night sky and wondered about the meaning and purpose of life. This book was written to reveal the meaning and purpose of our: lives, struggles, sufferings, joys, and the origins of sin and evil that create such suffering.

A prince in the sixth century BC left the comfort of royalty in search of enlightenment. Once he reached enlightenment by seeking answers to many of life's mysteries, he taught his realization for another forty-five years until his death. He taught that humanity has two natures. One is our ordinary nature or ego self, which is made up of feelings such as jealousy, hatred, and fear. The other is our true nature, which is pure consciousness and love.

Those who are not enlightened, he believed, have not awakened to their true nature. He traveled around India teaching that the origin of our suffering was our ignorance of our true nature. He became known as the Buddha, which means the Awakened One.

While Josie and I surely don't consider ourselves Buddhas, this book was born out of our own questions about the mysteries of life and our search into these mysteries. Ironically, it was asking the same question that brought us together in this joint venture: Is there life after death? Josie and I may not agree on everything, but we both know without a doubt that life does not end.

As I look back on my life, it is evident that I have always thought about life and death. Since I was a child, I have always feared death. It seemed too farfetched that we could have an invisible soul that goes on to another world after we die physically. I felt this was simply wishful thinking.

I grew up with no strong religious ties, and on the surface I appeared to be more of a materialist than anything else (i.e., believing the physical world is all there is to reality). Yet, truthfully, I cannot say that I was an atheist, as something inside kept telling me that there must be more to life than our five senses can perceive. Outwardly, however, I considered myself invincible, and I repressed thoughts about my own death.

I led a successful life as a consultant, training employees in management and process improvement methodologies and making a very good living. I was on autopilot and didn't look back until something forced me to change my way of life. After experiencing some health problems, I visited a physician, who sent me to a specialist, who then led me to believe that my condition was serious and I would likely not live much longer. My egotistical concrete walls came crashing down on me as I realized I was not immune to the inevitable. I, too, would die someday.

Thankfully, the doctor proved to be completely wrong in his diagnosis. But it did not matter, because I was never the same again. At nearly fifty years of age, I realized that I knew little about the mysteries of life, and thus began my journey, which now has lasted more than two decades as I have delved into the answers to the mysteries of life. My quest was insatiable; I began my search by studying near-death experiences and then everything from Buddhism to Hinduism to Metapsychiatry to quantum physics to spiritualism and the teachings of Jesus and the mystics.

As a consultant, I taught root cause and effect analysis in my seminars by asking *why* questions several times to seek beyond the symptoms of an effect. I discovered that the Buddha was right when he said the origin of suffering was ignorance. If so, then what is the origin of this ignorance that causes so much, if not all, of the suffering in the world? I could not find anything on the origin of ignorance, so I posed this question to anyone and everyone who would listen.

For stress relief and relaxation, I would go up into the Arizona Mountains to ride my trail bike and take long walks in the forest. I was very skeptical of religious beliefs and doubted that consciousness survived physical death. Even though I considered myself atheist/agnostic, and I thought God might be in the same category as Santa Claus and the Easter Bunny, I started to pray on my hands and knees. I asked to be shown the other side. I wanted some sort of proof that there was more to my existence than the physical. Material success had done little to bring me the peace and happiness I sought. So I felt I had no choice but to try to seek the help of a higher source, if indeed a higher source existed.

For several years, I continued to travel to the mountains for peace, relaxation, and to pray. Then, finally, my answers came in 1990 over a two-week period in the most unlikely of places: my dreams. In fact, I had not one but three vivid dreams. The first two consisted of being shown beauty and nature beyond mere words. The forests were a beautiful vibrant green, and the lakes were a brilliant bluish green. I floated effortlessly about one hundred yards above the ground, witnessing the incredible beauty below. I later learned that I had experienced what are often called garden dreams, during which we are shown the astral world, or what some refer to as a garden paradise.

The third dream was so profound that not a day goes by that I don't think about it. A woman came to me who looked to be about forty-five years old; she wore a light gray gown that paled in comparison to her shoulder length, light gray hair. She stood about ten feet away from me, and we looked intently into each other's eyes. I stood there mesmerized by her radiant smile as we engaged in telepathic communication. No words were spoken, nor did there need to be, as she knew everything there was to know about me. It was instantaneous. She had perfect understanding of all my past and present feelings, emotions, and thoughts. She knew what I had done and why I had done it—even the most selfish acts that I had committed. Absolutely nothing I had ever done was hidden from her, yet she did not judge me or condemn me—I felt only total acceptance and love from her.

This entity then opened her arms as I floated toward her effortlessly. When our bodies touched, we both shared an unearthly vibration that was pure ecstasy. After this incredible spiritual hug, the dream or vision ended, but its effect will be with me forever. I will never forget the total acceptance that I received from this most compassionate woman with the sweetest of smiles. It was beyond any feeling I have ever experienced on earth. The best I can do is to say that I felt a kind of ecstasy that surpasses my ability to describe.

This dream, with its telepathic communication and spiritual hug, gave me the passion to seek deeper into the mysteries of life. Ironically, or maybe not so ironically, a dream is how it all began for Josie Varga as well. What follows is her account of what happened:

> *The epilogue of my first book, Footprints in the Sand: A Disabled Woman's Inspiring Journey to Happiness, contains an inspirational e-mail written by my husband's friend and former boss, Rich, who died during the World Trade Center attacks on September 11. In it, Rich talks about the passing of his father, but more so about the importance of life. After completion of this book, Rich came to me in a vivid dream that seemed more real than dream-like; it forever changed my view of the afterlife, and it strengthened my faith in God.*
>
> *In the dream, I saw myself going through a long hall-way. I had no idea where I was, yet there seemed to be a force pushing me forward, as I made my way to the end of the hallway, I turned right into a door at the end. I walked into this room and looked around, seeing a bunch of desks and windows. I should also mention here that I actually felt myself moving. It was as though my soul was out wandering while my body remained in a deep sleep. All of a sudden, Rich appeared before me. He was wearing glasses, and he smiled reassuringly at me as he telepathically communicated, "Josie, thank you for mentioning me in your book."*
>
> *I had never met Rich in person when he was alive on this earth. I had only spoken to him on the phone, and I knew what he looked like through pictures I had seen of him, yet I had no doubt that this was my husband's friend standing before me. I looked up at him, squinting because it was hard to look straight at him. The only reason I can give for this is there seemed to be a density or fog about us. To this day, I don't know why I said this, but I looked at him and said, "Rich, you have to give me proof that this is really you." He looked at me with a comforting glance,*

and then he walked over to a desk and picked up a cell phone. On the cell phone was a picture of him, his wife, and his son.

He then spoke to me again and said, "Boston is OK." I had no idea what this meant, but the next thing I knew I was going through a window and found myself on the street looking up at a pickup truck. In the bed of this pickup truck was Rich standing behind his wife and son. He looked at me and told me to give them the message. I don't remember anything much after that except for waking up panting and sweating in a sitting position and feeling like something had just hit me in my chest.

I must admit I was scared and confused. Nothing like this had ever happened to me before. Though I could not understand what had just happened, I was certain that I had to get this message to his wife. It was about eight in the morning and my husband was already at work. I quickly rushed to call John and told him what had just happened. His response was nothing that I didn't expect. "You've got to be kidding me," he yelled. "You want me to call Rich's wife, who just lost her husband, and tell her that 'Boston is OK'?" He was convinced that I had lost my senses.

I persisted, telling him that I was positive the experience had been real and not a dream. It had been unlike anything that I had ever experienced. As I would later find out, I had just experienced a form of out-of-body experience (OBE) known as astral travel. When this occurs, the soul leaves the physical body to travel in its astral body to other dimensions or realms of reality. My husband listened reluctantly but finally agreed to forward to Rich's sister-in-law an e-mail written by me, explaining what had occurred. He would ask her to forward the e-mail to Rich's wife only if she felt it was appropriate to do so.

The following week, we were on vacation when my husband received a response from Rich's sister-in-law on his BlackBerry. In short, she explained that her sister had a brother in Boston and was considering moving there. However, having purchased her home just before her husband's untimely death, she felt guilty. My husband read this message to himself but did not grasp what the message meant until he read the e-mail aloud to me.

We both looked at each other in complete shock. I had never met Rich's wife and certainly did not know that she even had a brother in Boston. Now, it all made perfect sense to me. Rich's words, "Boston is OK," were meant to let his wife know that she need not feel guilty and should move to Boston. He was telling her that it was all right with him.

At first, I honestly did not know what to think. A deceased friend had given me a message in my dreams that had actually been validated. What next? What did this mean? Even though I had no doubt that I had visited with Rich's spirit and that he was alive and well, my ego self had difficulty processing this information. While my unconditioned self or spirit believed that what I had experienced was perhaps more real than anything I had witnessed on this earth, my ego self was afraid and doubtful. After all, I reasoned, if Rich is dead and if he did, in fact, communicate with me, then not only was it confirmation of the existence of an afterlife, but it must be possible for the dead to communicate with the living.

I did not realize it then, but this experience would ultimately lead me on a spiritual quest, which would result in two books: Visits from Heaven and Visits to Heaven. Life will never be the same. What a gift it is to no longer fear death.

Over the past twenty-two years, I have asked myself many questions. For instance, if our true nature is pure consciousness and love, then what is love? What is the purpose of life? The vivid dream experience I had with the spirit being in the light gray gown (I have since learned that the spiritualists call it a "visitation") forever changed my perception of reality and life. I was never the same because I realized after much reflection that what I was experiencing in this life was only a shadow of the love available to us. We are asleep to the reality of our spiritual love.

Looking back, I now believe that the radiant, accepting woman in light-gray grown was my guide or soul mate, but I like to call her my guardian angel because of the indescribable love and acceptance she showed me. At one time, I felt that the idea of a soul mate was ridiculous, but this visitation from another world changed my view of reality. I have learned that as we travel through these lifetimes as different personalities (egos), and in the astral world as souls, we often share human experiences and events with those who have been with us for hundreds or even thousands of years. (We will talk more about reincarnation later in this book.)

We have all met someone and felt an immediate, unexplainable connection; it appears that we have known him or her before. Well, maybe we have. Souls are said to exist between lives in groups (soul clusters) of other souls. These souls create a loving bond that keeps them together for centuries. So, again, getting back to my dream, I felt as though I already knew this woman. There was a deep, unquestionable bond between us.

When I awoke from this dream, I began my spiritual quest, which I now believe I was meant to take. Ironically, I had knowledge that I didn't even know I had. My spiritual journey began in full force. Words and thoughts poured out so naturally, yet at times I had no idea where they came from. Hence, this led to many discoveries. Among them, I realized that there are three profound questions about the mysteries of life:

1. What is the origin of suffering?

2. What is the origin of ignorance?

3. What is the meaning of creation?

I have learned that most people don't even know that these questions exist. How many times have you been asked to explain the origin of ignorance or the meaning of creation? I'd be willing to bet your answer is never. Yet, until we solve these mysteries, we will continue to place blame when it comes to our suffering.

We have all at one time or another asked, "Why me, God?" We've blamed everything and everyone for our suffering, including God. Well, God is not responsible for your suffering and neither are you. What, then, is the origin of suffering, and who exactly is God?

This last question may seem like an absurd one to ask. God has been called many things—Yahweh, Almighty, Jehovah, Allah, Absolute Being, and Supreme or Cosmic Consciousness, to name a few. Do you ever wonder why there are so many descriptions of God? One answer is because God cannot really be defined. *God is infinite, and to define the concept of infinity is to limit it, because infinity has no boundaries; therefore, it cannot be defined.*

You will find the answers to these profound questions and more in this book. Keep in mind that if we don't ask the right questions, we seldom get the right answers, and by *right*, I mean *valid*. A valid question has the opportunity to reveal a valid answer. Notice I said *opportunity*, because there are no guarantees that asking the right question will always reveal to us the right answer. Oftentimes, our conditioned beliefs and ego-centered biases can create a mental paralysis that has the ability to filter all incoming information and make us blind to the truth that we seek.

This book was written with the intention of teaching a valid concept of God's attributes. These help us to see the underlying reality of the relative-phenomenal world. The relative world gives us variation, and the phenomenal world gives us unique experiences as opportunities for growth in our soul's awareness of reality. A valid perception of God's attributes helps us to evaluate phenomena beyond appearances. An invalid concept or perception of God is the belief that God is capable of anger, wrath, and jealousy, and that God demands to be worshiped, has chosen people and nations, believes in human sacrifice, and has given humans the free will to separate themselves from Oneness.

It is my hope that this book will help readers to remove these so-called blinders and awaken to better knowledge and understanding of these three mysteries of life. I do realize that some readers may reject this book as heresy, but even in rejection, there is involvement. There is so much more to this world than meets the eye.

As Saint Paul said, "So we fix our eyes not on what is seen, but on what is unseen. For the things which are seen are temporal; but the things which are not seen are eternal" (2 Corinthians 4:18 NIV). As divine expressions of God, we are all part of the Creator; we are all eternal souls.

PARADIGMS:
A MIXED BLESSING

"Real knowledge is to know the extent of one's ignorance."
—Confucius

A paradigm is a mental model of how we view our world. We literally view the physical world through our inner world of beliefs and paradigms. Paradigms are often confused with beliefs, but this is in error. We are often willing to share the beliefs we cherish, whether others want to hear about them or not, but our paradigms are hidden from our view. They act as filters or gateways, influencing our views of reality moment by moment at a subconscious level.

The mixed blessing of paradigms is that information or evidence that agrees with our hidden paradigm finds an easy path to recognition, but information or evidence that disagrees with our paradigm hits a brick wall of denial on the path to recognition. This explains why paradigm shifts are very rare. One of the best examples of a paradigm shift is when Galileo discovered with his telescope that the earth was not the center of our solar system. He paid a heavy price for revealing his discovery to the religious leaders of his day, who had a mental model (paradigm) that the earth was the center of the universe.

While reading this book, you might find yourself having thoughts such as, *Everybody knows that adults should know right from wrong,* or *Everybody knows that sin and evil exist as a reality,* and so on.

If you have such thoughts, ask yourself this question: Who is everybody? *Everyone* believed that the earth

11

was flat and the center of the universe for thousands of years. Almost *everyone* in Switzerland believed with absolute certainty that watches would always be made of mechanical springs and jewel bearings. How many of us can remember when we would go to a jewelry store and the jeweler would remove the back of the watch to show us those beautiful twenty-one-jewel bearings?

Until the nineteenth century, *everyone* believed that the atom was the smallest particle in existence. *Everyone* believed that heavier objects fall faster than lighter objects. Even Aristotle got that one wrong. Almost everyone believes that Napoleon was short, but research has shown that he was about average height for males in the early nineteenth century.

Everyone believed that radar could detect any moving object, such as an airplane, until a Russian scientist wrote a paper on stealth technology. Almost *everyone*, including the leading scientists, believed that heavier-than-air flight was impossible. *Everyone* who is a confirmed materialist believes with certainty that paranormal phenomena are impossible. The list is long of *everyone* who believed what he or she thought was impossible, only to be proved possible later.

During the American Revolutionary War, *everyone* in the English army lined up in his bright red uniform, stood shoulder to shoulder with members of his regiment, and marched straight toward the enemy's barrage of gunfire. Today's military paradigm would call that a suicide march, but it was the cherished military paradigm of the English army. It is interesting to note that most people do not believe that we could make these same kinds of mistakes today. This belief is shortsighted and naïve because it fails to understand the power of the paradigm effect.

These are just a few examples of the way that long-held beliefs create the paradigm effect, which tells us that what we believe is fact. If a new paradigm is introduced, the world rejects it outright before investigation and most often even before any conscious consideration is given to its veracity. The most prevailing examples of paradigms are in the realms of religion, politics, and, surprisingly, science. Buckminster Fuller stated, "You never change things by fighting the existing reality. To change something, build a new model that makes the existing model obsolete."

We are introducing in this book a new mental model: a paradigm shift from the world's paradigm of humankind's fallen status, which many call original sin, to that of original innocence. We will show why the existing world's paradigm of humanity in the grips of human blameworthiness and original sin is in error. By all appearances, original sin and human culpability comprise a valid model of humanity, but appearances can be deceiving: to paraphrase Jesus, judge not by appearances, but judge by righteous judgment.

Our new model is a God of unconditional love and infinite awareness that did not err by creating humans who would choose sin and evil over love by eating from the tree of the knowledge of good and evil. Seeking knowledge and understanding is the soul's evolutionary journey to greater and greater levels of love and divine intelligence. God, the Infinite Oneness of "all that is," is the creative source and process of manifesting *varying* expressions of its infinite potential. Two interesting definitions of *varying* are *to change in form, appearance, and substance,* and *to give variety to.*

The new paradigm offered in this book will answer an age-old question: If God is perfect and unconditional love, then why is it that we humans cannot demonstrate this perfect love in our lives? Infinite Awareness by its very definition must know past, present, and future, and this book will build a new paradigm of the origin of our suffering, the origin and purpose of our unawareness (i.e., ignorance), and the meaning and purpose of creation.

Our paradigm is not built upon beliefs or wishful thinking, but on an understanding of the necessity of a relative-phenomena world for Infinite Oneness that has the perfect awareness to express its attributes of love and divine intelligence. A relative world demands variation, which is the act, process, or result of a change in form, appearance, and substance, and that variation of awareness within each and every soul is an absolute necessity for creation to occur.

The underlying reality of all variation within the infinite awareness of God is some level or degree of unawareness that we view as imperfections. The soul's learning process over time and experiences with its created imperfections are what make it unique. Imperfections in our character and values are but degrees of unawareness, and a synonym for unawareness is ignorance. *Ignorance* and *ignore* have the same Latin root, and one definition of *ignore* is *to be unaware*. Our souls were created unaware as a divine necessity, because without our original unawareness, there is no us; there is only the stillness of Isness (i.e., God).

It is interesting to note that we humans view our limited awareness as imperfection, but God views it as a creation process of perfectly imperfect unawareness. This ability to view unawareness as perfect in its imperfection requires an understanding that unawareness is a necessity to create unique souls. This understanding is at the very heart of our original and eternal innocence. Therefore, when a soul becomes more advanced in love and divine intelligence, that soul demonstrates greater compassion and love toward all of humanity.

What we see as the imperfections of humanity, God sees as the perfection of our unawareness. How can this be? How can God see perfection in our imperfections?

God sees the underlying reality of our imperfections. All the imperfections of the human character that we term as sin and evil have one thing in common: unawareness of our perfect and divine reality. Without these imperfections, there is no *us* as individualized souls; there is only perfect awareness, which is God.

Given time and experiences, each soul develops as a unique expression of God. This is why we have included a chapter on prerequisites, which will help the reader see through the filters that society has conditioned us to accept concerning the very essence of our being, which is spirit.

While reading the next chapter "Prerequisites" always keep in mind, if one has a longing to become a sincere seeker into the mysteries of life, he must seek beyond many of the world's established beliefs. This is extremely difficult to do because our religious or atheist beliefs have become our <u>hidden</u> paradigm paralysis.

A starting point to help overcome this paradigm effect is to state often early in our search, "I know I don't know". The ego will scream in protest and cause much mental suffering, as it wants to be known for knowing. During our seeking into these mysteries of life, there is a human tendency to want quick results. We may accept many existing and often invalid established religious and societal beliefs.

PREREQUISITES

"Since it is all too clear, it takes time to grasp it."
—Zen saying

After years of attempting to explain my discoveries to others, I wondered why there was such resistance and/or lack of understanding of my words. It came to me that there are several prerequisites for these discoveries to be understood. With this in mind, I would like to explain what I believe is necessary for a person to begin to have knowledge of these three mysteries.

Many have called my writing style "PhD speak," among other terms, so I will try to stay on point and write about the prerequisites in a manner that makes sense to the reader. Personal experiences with awareness and humility are the best teacher, so if I can relate my words to the readers' experiences, then maybe these discoveries will make more sense.

God: First, we need a definition of God, even though we must fully realize that we cannot completely define God. God is infinite; there is no other source of all creation. Infinite and Perfect Awareness is the best definition that I can give to this Infinite Source of all that is. The word *awareness* is critical, as most want to think of God as some kind of supreme or superhuman mega cosmic consciousness. Remember, we humans have a tendency to make God in our image with human traits and behaviors.

By *awareness*, I do not mean just simple observation or witnessing; I mean the ability to see the underlying reality of all that is. This is one aspect of spiritual discernment. There is a fundamental difference between awareness and consciousness. Awareness is stillness, not nothingness, or emptiness as many religious gurus teach. Awareness is timelessness; consciousness is a flow of thoughts or a series of thoughts that require a time-based perceived reality. Events and experiences occur in our lives in a serialized format (one experience, then another), and this serial approach to existence requires a time-based perceived reality.

The necessity of time: *Time is not an illusion but rather is a perceived necessity for the creation of unique expressions (souls) of God to exist.*

When our consciousness evolves to higher levels of awareness, we live in the present in a perceived timeless-based reality, which is more blissful and joyful. Most of our fears are the result of past events that we relive in our minds and future events that we worry will occur. Stated another way, about 99 percent of what we worry about due to our fears is unfounded.

Most of those fears dwell in our desire to control and our lack of trust in the perfection of the Absolute to expand and develop our consciousness to greater awareness. Learning to trust in the universal law of cause and effect is very difficult. It is natural that we want to control our lives. It is normal and expected at this phase of our evolution-of-consciousness process called physical life to be unable to see the perfection of a loving God. Our level of trust increases as our awareness expands.

The difference between awareness and observation can be explained by the following example. If we go out on a clear day and look up into the sky, we see space, lots of space; this is an act of observation with some degree of awareness. We observe the blue sky, the leaves of the trees moving in the wind, and any plane that might be flying overhead.

Quantum physicists tell us that we are only seeing a small percentage of the reality that exists in the universe. The much larger reality is hidden in dark matter and energy that might be better called unaware or unknown matter and energy. Therefore, we are aware of only a small portion of what exists in the universe. This limited perception is due to our limited awareness of all the realities that exist in our universe. God, with perfect or infinite awareness, is aware of all reality. According to the Bible, Jesus said that God is aware of every hair on our heads.

Every thought, every experience, and every event in our lives has meaning, and the more aware we become; the more we begin to see the underlying meanings of our thoughts and experiences and those of others. With simple observation, we only see and experience drama, and often we feel like victims, but with expanded awareness, we see these meanings and underlying realties of this drama that we call human life. This level of sincere seeking is another aspect of spiritual discernment.

Our awareness is limited; if our awareness were not limited, we would be God, with perfect awareness. With observation, we are using our limited awareness to experience our reality. As our consciousness advances, our awareness increases and expands. With consciousness, there is always a duality of them and us, but with awareness, there is greater understanding that we as souls are not separate from God. It is very important to understand the difference between consciousness and awareness in order to understand the mysteries of life presented in this book.

Space is not empty. It appears empty to us because of our limited awareness or our lack of awareness of it. There is no space, void, or nothingness in the mind of Infinite Awareness; the perception of space is only in our limited awareness of it. What we observe as space is full of vitality and substance. Scientists are calling this vitality and substance dark energy and dark matter because of their materialistic paradigm. Space is nonexistent to the Mind that has infinite or pure awareness.

It is important to note here that our limited awareness is what makes us unique souls and thus distinguishable from God. Limited awareness is not a sin, but it is troublesome. This is why we as souls have the capacity to expand our awareness and draw ever closer to God's divine love and intelligence. We were not created with perfect awareness but with unawareness and innocence. In our innocence, we often err or miss the target.

Our imperfections are not a mistake made by our Creator but a necessity to create unique souls. To blame our imperfections on our human condition is to miss the real root meaning of the word responsibility as the ability to respond. It is our created imperfections (i.e. unawareness) that make us distinguishable from this Infinite Source we call God. We cannot take personal responsibility for our imperfections. To blame ourselves for our imperfections is based in ignorance, not awareness. God does not duplicate; God creates, and what is infinite must create less than perfect souls as a form of limited awareness in its creation.

Spiritual truth: *Creation beyond duplication demands some level or origin of unawareness.*

We are humans with eternal souls, and we lack complete understanding of the consequences of our thoughts and actions. We are learning, and often we experience very harsh lessons in life. In the physical realm of existence, those lessons are frequently not only mental suffering, but physical lessons of pain and suffering.

When my son was about seven years old, we took a group trip to Six Flags, and during that day at Six Flags, my son wandered off, which he did often. The group and I looked for him for hours. My fears of something horrible happening to him grew by the minute.

I still remember that moment when I first saw him wandering in the bleachers, looking like he had not a care in the world, as if he had become separate from the group just minutes ago. My first instinct was profound relief that the son I loved deeply was safe and unharmed. Of course, I did inform him of the time we had spent looking for him, and I told him never to wander off again.

My point is that he lacked understanding that his actions could have had severe consequences for him. He was inexperienced in the lessons of life and their consequences. A synonym for inexperience is innocence. In our innocence, we often miss the target, and one definition of sin is missing the target.

My son was still a child, but even for adults who probably know right from wrong, knowing is profoundly different from understanding. As my friend often states, "We can know it but not do it." This book will explain that we can miss the target and wander off for a variety of reasons. As souls, we were purposely created inexperienced and blameless, and with purity and innocence, for divine reasons.

Something to reflect on often is the idea that God is a dynamic God, and creation beyond duplication demands some level or origin of unawareness. If souls were created with perfect awareness, they would not be expressions of God but rather duplications of God. Infinite Oneness cannot be duplicated.

Spiritual truth: *Infinite Oneness cannot be duplicated but it can be expressed.*

As souls, we have almost infinite lessons to learn as we advance in awareness on our unique paths to becoming more perfect and unique expressions of God. As our perfection in awareness grows, we become more loving and intelligent. Both of these aspects of soul development bring us greater joy, bliss, and love for God, self, and others.

This process-oriented awakening is the journey of the soul, and the journey of all souls becomes the vibrant expression of a dynamic, loving, creative, and all-knowing God. In other words, the best is yet to come as our understanding of our divine reality grows in awareness.

Infinity is timeless. There is no such thing as time in pure awareness. This difference between timeless awareness and the relative nature of consciousness is critical if we are to understand the three mysteries that have plagued humankind since the dawn of the human intellect. We must understand that in this world and these other dimensions or worlds that souls reside in, all souls have degrees of unawareness. We do not instantly know all there is to know after we cross over. We arrive at our new homes as our same sweet selves, or not-so-sweet selves, depending on our levels of consciousness and awareness.

Often we hear people talk about the difference between spirituality and religion. Religion is based on beliefs, whereas spiritual understanding or spirituality is based on awareness. The more aware we are, the more spiritual we become in our daily lives. An atheist can be very spiritual without being religious. Most atheists confuse religion with spirituality and think they are the same. I have known many atheists who are more spiritual than many religious people I know or have read about.

As we become more aware of various phenomena in our daily lives, we begin to see the underlying reality of all experiences. This increase in awareness gives greater meaning and purpose to life. Often, religious beliefs can become a handicap to greater awareness as beliefs can overwhelm the infinite love that is constantly attempting to blend with our flow of thoughts.

It is very important to ask yourself why such hatred can be seen in the world if we have an infinite sea of loving thoughts available to us. The explanation lies in the lower levels of awareness that exist within our personal consciousness. Think of a human soul as an aspect of Perfect Awareness that most call God. Because we are aspects of God, we must be created with limited awareness. (More on this later in the book as the difference between limited awareness and infinite awareness reveals the difference between God and God's creation.)

I have spent much time in this book writing about the subtle difference between awareness and consciousness. This difference is not easy to comprehend, but doing so is necessary in order to understand the mysteries of life that have troubled humankind since the dawn of the soul. For now, while reading this book, think of consciousness as the flow of thoughts that pass through our individual minds, and think of awareness as the ability to see reality.

The first prerequisite to understanding the three mysteries of life is realizing that God can best be defined as Perfect Awareness, Absolute, Infinite Awareness, whereas a soul is a conscious being having both consciousness and limited but expanding awareness.

Infinite: The next prerequisite is the concept of the infinite. We have defined God as Infinite Awareness, but we also need to define an operational definition of what is *infinite*. Infinite is All in All, timelessness, and without boundaries. Many dictionaries define *infinite* as *endless*, but it is more than endless; it had no beginning. If anything lies outside of infinite, then what we thought was infinite is not. There is no beginning or ending to infinity. Without perfect awareness, the mind cannot fathom infinity.

We desperately want infinity to have a beginning just as our souls had a beginning. We want to make this Infinite Awareness in our image. We cannot visualize this Infinite Source as all that is, but we can come to know and be aware of the Source of all that is. This is the journey of the soul from limited awareness to greater awareness. The more awareness we attain, the closer we get to God. The closer we get to God, the more love, compassion, divine intelligence, and creativity we have.

The more spiritually aware we become, the more we see that we are made in the image and likeness of this Infinite Awareness that most call God. It is easier said than done to comprehend that this Infinite Awareness is Absolute Oneness. There is no multiplicity (variation) to Oneness. Oneness is All in All; absolutely nothing lies outside of Oneness. Oneness is infinite, and infinite is Oneness.

If we cannot understand that Infinite Awareness and Oneness are the same, we cannot possibly see the causal connection between God and its creation of souls. We will continue to make God in our image until we understand the difference in awareness between the Creator as the source of all creation and its creation.

We as humans with eternal souls have boundaries, but there are no boundaries or limitations to Infinite Oneness, except one. That limitation gets very deep, very fast: *Oneness must create within its infinite awareness and vitality.* If nothing can exist outside of infinity, as there are no boundaries to infinity, then creation must exist within this Infinite Oneness. This concept is rejected by most religions because most religious people want to make God in their image.

Most religions want to put God somewhere out there in the universe separate from humans here on Earth. This is because we want to be separate beings in charge of our own destiny and lives. To maintain our personal identity, we believe we must feel separate from our Creator. This is a natural part of the evolution of the soul. Every soul has to go through this stage of development. This evolution-of-the-soul process is as much a part of creation as the big bang.

We should not condemn our lack of awareness; instead, we must obtain greater awareness of our potential. We were created in the image of God; we are not perfect like God. If we were created perfect, there would be no us; only God. That would not be creation but duplication of Oneness, and of course Oneness cannot be duplicated, just as infinite cannot be duplicated.

God made in the image of man is easier to preach about and visualize for followers of all religions. How can one visualize perfect awareness and the infinite? How can one visualize perfect love? How can one describe a rose in all of its beauty to a person who has been blind since birth? We all have degrees of blindness within the limitations of our awareness. There is a very good spiritual reason for our limited awareness, or, as the title of this book states, our soul's original innocence.

The ego or human mind, even the mind of the soul, desperately wants to make God in its image because it fears losing its identity. It is impossible to lose one's identity. Our identity will change over a series of events in our lives, but a change of identity does not mean a loss of identity. We do not have the same identity today that we had yesterday. This is important to consider, because the ego is so fragile that it might find a justification for not finishing this book if it believes that doing so will cause it to lose its identity. In fact, the human ego feels that its very existence depends on being deceptive.

To state this in another way, we are constantly changing. Something that I experience today will make me a different person tomorrow. The spiritualists call this the law of progress. What looks like bad may actually be good. No matter what we go through in life, it develops our soul.

The human ego's need to be deceptive is based in the fear of its nonexistence or loss of identity. This fear causes the fragile ego to affirm itself constantly and to seek recognition in a multitude of different and often self-destructive ways. The ego is not to be condemned for this deception, for we must always move beyond condemnation and seek understanding of this need for deception.

The underlying fear that every soul must experience on its journey from believing it is a separate entity from God to an expression of Infinite Oneness is part of the process of the evolution of the soul. This process of experiences, choices, and fate creates in every soul a unique expression of Infinite Oneness.

Many profound thinkers use the analogy that God is the painter, and the painting is God's creation. It's a nice analogy, but it fails on two fronts: it fails to understand Oneness as All in All, and it fails to understand the concept of the infinite. This analogy makes God in man's image. Man can create a painting outside of himself, but God, being All in All, has to create a painting within its own Oneness. With God as the painter, the painting and the painter are from the same source: Infinite Oneness. It is critical that we understand why this painter analogy makes God in man's image.

We want to tell others that God is All in All, and then, in the very next breath, we want to tell people that God can create outside its infinite All in All. At this stage of our evolutionary journey as souls, we feel separate from God, so naturally we desire to have a God that can create us as separate beings from our creator. We feel separate from God and all others for a very good and spiritual reason—actually, a reason that will be explained later in this book.

The Relationship of Awareness and Consciousness:
I have alluded to these in previous paragraphs, and both are indescribable and considered by atheists and scientific materialists as a hard problem because they cannot find the center for consciousness in the brain. Every cell in the body has some level of consciousness. Most people consider awareness just a by-product of consciousness. It certainly looks that way, but appearances and feelings can be very deceptive.

We are living beings who demonstrate our very existence consciously; this consciousness reveals itself to us as a flow of thoughts during meditation, whereas awareness reveals itself to us as understanding. We choose our thoughts, often on a subconscious level, depending on our level of awareness. The quality of our thoughts reflects our awareness of reality. Awareness is more than perception. Perception is observation with different degrees of awareness.

Our awareness is less than perfect, as we were not created perfect. The reason for this is one of the great mysteries revealed in this book. Only Oneness is perfect, and this Oneness can be described as Infinite or Perfect Awareness.

We are like ants attempting to understand what lies beyond our anthill; it is far beyond our understanding. We live in fear of being nothingness but refuse to admit to others our greatest fear: nonexistence. Most of us live very stoic lives, repressing horrible thoughts that we may not have personal identities beyond this life. These fears and our attempts to live stoic lives often reveal themselves as neurotic and psychotic behaviors.

We suffer, and we see ignorance all around us, but we refuse to admit our own ignorance. We ponder the meaning and purpose of our lives. These were the concerns and questions I had two decades ago when I began to seek answers. The journey has not been an easy one, and it is ongoing, but there is no better and more challenging research than the mysteries of life.

The world is often called dualistic: the belief that the world consists of two separate and primary entities. Many sages and most religious leaders teach this concept. The world appears to us as dualistic, but appearances are deceiving. For example, there appears to be hot/cold, good/bad, and God/us, but there is variation in all things except the Absolute. There are many degrees of water temperature between hot and cold. Maybe there are infinite degrees of variation between what we perceive as good and bad.

There is not a God out there in space somewhere. Rather, there is God, and within God's unbounded and never-ending Oneness is creation, which contains an infinite variety of life forms. One of the keys to understanding this relative-phenomenal world is to understand its meaning and purpose. Everything in this world has meaning; indeed, even every thought has meaning. We create the fallacy that our world is dualistic because we judge by appearances. We also propagate this belief so that we can feel separate from God. At this stage in our evolution-of-the-soul process, a separate identity is of utmost important to us.

The need for separation is a normal part of our evolutionary journey. Many so-called enlightened writers will try to convince their readers that it is very egotistical and dreadful to have such feelings of dualism and the desire to be separate and special. They do so without realizing that it is as much a part of the journey of the soul for a human as breathing air is.

Every snowflake that has ever fallen upon the earth is unique. There are not just large snowflakes and small snowflakes; every flake has some degree of variation in its intricate pattern and design, and sometimes this can be seen without a microscope.

Just as every snowflake is unique, so is every soul. Similarly, the relative-phenomenal world is a necessity for the creation of unique souls. It is critical that we understand this aspect of the relative-phenomenal world if we are to understand the meaning and purpose of creation.

If every grain of sand, every snowflake, every star, and every soul is unique, this means that the process of creating such phenomena has infinite intelligence. It did not occur by chance, as some would have us believe. This uniqueness stems from a process that does not duplicate itself in its creation. The Absolute has no need or desire to duplicate itself or its creation. The Absolute has a necessity to express itself in an infinite variety of forms.

Everything in the universe was created to sustain life. In physics, the anthropic principle was founded in response to a series of realizations that the laws of nature as we know them are remarkably consistent and precise in order to allow conditions for life. According to Wikipedia, "This phenomenon is actually a necessity because living observers wouldn't be able to exist, and hence observe the universe, were these laws and constants not constituted in this way."

For example, if the amount of oxygen in the air was slightly more or less than it is, we would not be able to breathe. Water freezes from the top and the ice floats. Ice is less dense than water (about 9 percent less). If this were not the case, living organisms could not exist in the water.

In the book *The Sermon on the Mount According to Vedanta*, Swami Prabhavananda states, "Variety and the unity of variety make up the uniform law of creation. Take away variety and the world would end." This is a statement about the necessity of a relative-phenomenal world for creation to occur. This quote is at the very essence of the original innocence of our divine nature. This variety is the result of an evolution-of-consciousness process (variety = variation = relativity) that makes every soul unique.

If perfection created perfect beings and not unique beings made in the image of God, we would be clones or duplicates. We are not duplicates of God but are varied and unique living beings made in the image of God to express the Infinite Source of all.

What exactly does being made in the image of God mean? It means we are spiritual beings having a human experience, and when we cross over to these other dimensions/worlds, we are spiritual beings having the experience of a soul or souls, which is our eternal reality.

Review of prerequisites:

1 God is Infinite Oneness.

2 God is Pure or Perfect Awareness, yet dynamic.

3 All consciousness has levels of awareness.

4 The greater our levels of awareness, the closer we are to the Absolute.

5 The closer we are to the perfection of the Absolute, the more love and joy we have in our lives.

6 The relative-phenomenal world is about variation, not dualism.

7 Our imperfections (unawareness) distinguish us from one another and our Creator.

8 Oneness must create within its infinite awareness and vitality.

THE MEANING OF SUFFERING

"I believe all suffering is caused by ignorance."
—Dalai Lama

Do we have to suffer? If every thought and action has meaning and purpose, than suffering has meaning and purpose. What if there were no consequences or feedback for our choices of love, compassion, hate, selfishness, greed, arrogance, and so on?

The meaning of suffering is that it can awaken and guide the soul to a greater love for self and others. Ask yourself, would a soul ever advance in love and divine intelligence without suffering? Most of us know that our struggles and hardships in life have given us a greater empathy for others. Empathy is on the path to compassion for all.

Suffering is an outcome of ignorance. This created unawareness is a necessity for the creation of unique souls to exist as infinite expressions of the oneness of God. The creation of unique souls is an evolution of consciousness process. That creation process is from the stillness of infinite awareness to the dynamic reality of relative-phenomenal worlds. If souls were created with perfect awareness, there would be no one-of-a-kind souls, only the stillness of perfect infinite awareness.

We want to take personal responsibility for our suffering because we have been told throughout our lives that we have been given free will and therefore we must take responsibility for 100 percent of our suffering due to the choices we make. This belief has been taught by parents, teachers, and most authority figures whether they are atheists or believers in God.

Do we really know the origin of our suffering, though? Most don't. In fact, my research has shown me that few in the world know the origin of suffering. Why is this? Why do people resist knowing something that is so profound and so available to be known? The answer has many aspects, or what the statisticians call significant variables or causes.

The simple answer is that we want to feel and be separate from this Absolute that most call God. Call it ego, pride, or whatever, but we really cherish our separateness and individuality. This feeling of separateness is normal and mandatory for the evolution of the soul to progress to greater levels of knowledge and divine intelligence. It is also normal and a necessity for God to express His infinite potential in a variety of expressions. Ask yourself what knowledge or understanding we lack that causes us to make misguided choices in life, which then cause us such suffering.

What is the opposite of understanding and knowledge? What is lack of knowledge? It is ignorance and unawareness, both of which cause most of our suffering. To put it simply, the origin of suffering is ignorance and unawareness. Because of our conditioned beliefs, our cherished beliefs, and our hidden paradigms, most of us resist the statement that the origin of our suffering is ignorance.

This resistance is normal and must be accepted as normal. We humans despise the word ignorance. We would much rather be called sinners and even evil than ignorant.

Look at the world around you. Billions of people are told every week that they are sinners. What is even more interesting is that some people will pay large sums of money to be told they are sinners. The ego takes to sin and guilt like a bird takes to flight. This happens because it is a form of self-confirmation that we are indeed separate from the Absolute Oneness. We live in fear of losing our personal identity.

This book is not about losing your personal identity. In fact, you will gain a greater sense of your identity than you have ever imagined. These fears are unfounded, as we are living souls, and we can and will become greater than we could ever envision.

Those who teach that the world is worthless and that rebirth should be avoided at all costs, and those who say that life has no meaning or purpose have failed to understand that human life is part of the journey of a soul. There is not just human life followed by nirvana due to an instant enlightenment; there is a progression and expansion of the soul's consciousness with a multitude of enlightened moments.

We are attaining an ongoing awareness of reality, which gives us a level of creative power that exceeds our ability to comprehend at this stage of our soul development and expansion. As expressions of the Most High, we will evolve to profound intelligence and creative abilities through an evolution-of-consciousness process. This process is the stuff of life. Physical bodies are mere garments for the evolving consciousness that is unfolding in each human soul.

Anyone who is not sincerely interested in seeking deeply into this evolution-of-consciousness process that is unfolding moment by moment is still very much unaware of divine reality. One way of evaluating one's consciousness development is by doing personal introspection and intellectual honestly, since this process takes us from sympathy for some to empathy for many to compassion for all.

When we attain knowledge of the evolution-of-consciousness process, we discover that consciousness never stops expanding in awareness toward the Infinite Source, which is the Perfect Awareness that most call God. This process is the evolution of the soul toward Infinite Oneness. This is our eternal innocence and our eternal reality as souls.

An attempt to judge reality by looking at one human life is akin to taking a snapshot of our soul's journey; this snapshot would be very misleading if it were presented as the complete picture of our journey. By all appearances we have fallen, disobeyed, and messed up ever since we were created, but appearances can be very deceiving. This system of beliefs concerning our fallen status gives little credit to our Creator, and it makes our Creator in the image of a human and thus imperfect and capable of making mistakes.

The divine perfection of God's awareness, intelligence, potential, and vitality is infinite; therefore, the progress of the soul is eternal. Think for a minute of a place you want to travel to, but it is an infinite distance. How long would it take you to arrive at such a place? Infinite is limitless. No matter how far you traveled, you would still have an infinite distance to travel.

The eternal progress of the soul may indeed be limitless; therefore, we can reason that the progress of our soul is ongoing and eternal. This limitless progression of the soul toward infinite awareness, intelligence, potential, and vitality makes every soul an eternal soul.

SPIRIT, EGO, AND GOD

Charles Darwin asked, "Have we any right to assume that the Creator works by intellectual powers like those of man?"

We all ask tough questions about life. In this twenty-first century, the religions of the world will be in the midst of many new discoveries regarding the origin of the universe and matters related to the mind, body, and soul. The ego will be unable to justify its existence as a separate reality from God, for it will finally realize its purpose and its connection to ultimate reality, which is spirit. We are eternal beings with a spirit essence. Our bodies are the garments we wear while on this earth plane.

The ego is comprised of our inner feelings and our consciousness of a separate self. The irony is that the evolution-of-the-soul process creates an ego with a perceived separate self. Then, as the soul advances in love and intelligence, that perceived separate self provides service and guidance to other souls that aren't as developed in their awareness of reality. We have much to learn about what the spiritualists call the law of progression.

Our conditioned self (ego) usually controls our lives and seeks recognition and eternity, sometimes at the expense of others and itself. While most Eastern religions and many New Thought religions appear to condemn the ego, I believe the ego is necessary to help us participate in the world. The wanting and not wanting misguided desires of the ego fuel our lifelong interest in this earthly experience, which teaches us divine lessons in spiritual awareness.

We spend most of our lives looking through our worldly ego's eyes. We believe we are our ego. We do not realize that we are a soul with a spark of divine spirit within us. Even our religions are ego based. But the good news is that we all have the capacity to see with our spirit eyes rather than our ego eyes as we renounce conditioned beliefs based in fear and seek the truth of our being.

It's easy to talk about the ego as though it is a separate entity with a mind of its own, but it's actually an aspect of the mind of God. Maybe it's best to think of the ego as the face of the soul that is revealing itself to the world. This face is often fearful and very selfish, especially when the soul is living a human life in a physical body. It is often in this state of mind or harsh physical environment that the soul can learn the most about itself and the mysteries of life.

Some have written about the many faces of God and its attributes, but there are many faces of the human mind and the mind of the soul as well. Those faces are often self-centered and selfish. That selfishness can lead to a whole host of problems, and the religious label it as sin; however, it is more accurate to state that sin is simply missing the mark. We were created in innocence of our true being, not in perfection, and in that innocence, it is inevitable that we will make mistakes and err in our judgment.

In this innocence, we develop a self-identity that can have relationships with others who are both less aware and more aware than we are. The journey and the expression of this Oneness that most call God would not be possible without our innocence. When that innocence is troublesome, we call it sin. Anyone who can see the underlying reality of phenomena that we call sin has profound awareness.

As humans, we can have relationships with one another, but God cannot have a relationship with another because the Oneness of infinite intelligence has no other to have a relationship with. Relationships have to have another, or at least the perception of other. The unawareness that is created in the creation process allows every soul to have a relationship with spouses, parents, children, cousins, and all others. This makes unawareness a divine and necessary aspect of the creation process.

We are not born on this earth as blank slates, but as physical bodies possessed by souls that have experienced many lives in order to advance in love and intelligence. When we blame all of our perceivably wrong choices on our dysfunctional childhood years or even on society, we fail to see the complexity of the human being.

When we question our core beliefs, our peace of mind is disturbed. The knowledge that we are not who we think we are can be emotionally upsetting. Religion and ego-centered beliefs can give us faith. This faith can be based on invalid assumptions, but faith in these invalid beliefs can help us cope with this world and our presence in it. Some believe it is better to have blind faith than no faith.

Two thousand years ago, Jesus said that he spoke in parables because we were blinded by our lack of understanding: "*Therefore, I speak to them in parables, because seeing they do not see, and hearing they do not hear, nor do they understand*" (Matthew 13:13, King James Version). In the Middle East, they have been quarreling over land and perceivably holy land for thousands of years. Surely, one can see the absurdity of fighting over a site thought to be holy. It is interesting to note that those doing the fighting on both sides consider themselves religious people, even to the point of believing that God has granted them special favors.

Only a God that has been given human traits would grant special favors to its creation. Perfection demands nothing less of a creator than love for all of its creation. We cannot say that God is perfect, and then say that God judges one group and has selected another to be its chosen people. These beliefs come from the ego, not the spirit.

The only judgment we receive during our time between lives is our own. It is our soul's journey to achieve perfection, and karma will bring us to that perfection. We are a collection of our thoughts and actions as a soul. The soul knows that it will have tremendous potential to learn while in the physical body.

The soul, our true essence or energy field, is what many refer to as our aura. This aura changes in color as we progress in divine intelligence. We were souls long before we were born. We are eternal beings because an Infinite Source of vitality and intelligence created us.

As humans, we experience this relative-phenomenal world in an infinite variety of ways. The relative world gives us variation, and the phenomenal world gives us temporal experiences (phenomena). Think of this world as a soul enhancer. Without it, where would a soul go to school? Plato, the great philosopher, once stated that with each new life a soul would drink from the River of Forgetfulness, so we are able to experience this world anew as a human.

The analogy that I like to use to explain this evolution-of-consciousness process is the polishing of a rock in a lapidary machine to which slurry has been added to create a polishing agent from the friction of the rocks rubbing together as they tumble in a container. When a stone first goes into this machine, it is usually very bland, but after a couple of days of rotating in this machine, it becomes a beautiful, polished stone. Our lapidary machine is the relative-phenomenal world, and our slurry is an almost infinite number of experiences that polish the soul into a magnificent beauty and reflection of God.

This universe might be described as an incubator for souls. Consciousness evolves. The whole cycle of life is the involution (i.e., involvement) of spirit: the creation process of many souls and the evolution of the soul to greater awareness. The soul has a tremendous advantage over the ego because most human souls have had many lives to learn many important lessons, such as the importance of love and compassion.

Souls are at all levels of evolution on Earth as well as in other dimensions, which most call the astral worlds. Jesus referred to these other worlds as "many mansions." These souls are not infinite but eternal; there is a big difference. The spirit dwells within the soul and is a fragment of God. This spirit is what sustains us with the lifeblood of our existence. Without it, we would cease to exist as consciousness and awareness.

The spirit within every soul creates a longing for completion. Because of the indwelling spirit within each soul, God shares perfect awareness with our soul. But because we have less-than-perfect intelligence, the soul fails to recognize its true nature. Whereas the soul is in the process of becoming perfection, the spirit already is.

If the spirit is part of God, then what is God? God is All in All. God is Perfect Awareness. God is Oneness—the Infinite Source of all that is. And if God is all that is, and we were created from this Isness or Oneness, then we must be part of the Creator. What then is the meaning of creation?

CREATION FROM ONENESS

"The possibility of life originating from accident is comparable to the probability of the unabridged dictionary resulting from an explosion in the printing shop."
—Edwin Conklin, biologist

In the previous chapter, we defined God as Oneness. This Oneness is both Infinite and Perfect Awareness. Each of us starts our journey as a spark of awareness that is an expression of God. You may wonder why God would not just create all souls with perfect awareness. Think of it this way: If perfection made us perfect souls, we would look back at our Creator and say to this Isness, "I am you." We would be duplicates of our Creator and would merge right back into this perfection.

Like attracts like, and Perfect souls would see no difference or uniqueness of character traits; therefore, there would be no interaction or expression. The perfection of God knows no variation except in its creation of imperfection. The very act of the creation process demands that every soul is created with original innocence.

During my journey of seeking truth, I was able to discover one of the great mysteries of life, and that is the relationship between creation, innocence, and ignorance. The Buddha was able not just to discover but also to realize the relationship of suffering and ignorance. When we accept that which the Buddha realized—that the origin of suffering is ignorance—then the next logical step is to question the origin of ignorance.

The Realization that Changed My Life

The origin of ignorance had remained a mystery until I fully understood the underlying reality of variation as it relates to the relative-phenomenal world. All variation has a level of ignorance or unawareness. If there were no variation, there would only be perfect awareness, and a synonym for perfect awareness is God. It is the necessity of variation for unique souls to be created. Synonyms for variation are *differences* and *distinctions*. Our inimitable distinctions make us unique souls, and without our differences, we would no longer exist as individualized beings. Without variation, there is only the stillness of Pure and Perfect Awareness.

As a successful business consultant teaching seminars in Continuous Improvement Mentality (CIM), I thought at first that this realization only helped me to understand the essence of leadership for organizations. Inherent in all organizations are systems (i.e., series of processes), and the larger the organization, the more systems it has, and often the more complex and demanding those systems become. Two kinds of variability of phenomena occur within any system: systemic and special causes of variation. If the leaders are to be effective, they must understand these two types of variation.

Systemic causes of variation are often called common, normal, or random causes of variation, but these terms are unrepresentative and often deceptive. There is nothing common, normal, or random about variation. All variation has meaning, just as all phenomena have meaning, so the terms common, normal, or random convey the idea of lacking purpose and meaning. This is what most quality experts miss, and furthermore, they often state that all variation is the enemy. The reality is that variation is our dearest friend;

indeed, it is the very essence of who we are as souls on a divine journey.

A variety of phenomena will communicate with us and guide us on our divine journey as souls if we are willing to listen to the signals these phenomena send to us every day of our lives. A special cause of variation is a signal that lies outside of what is normal or systemic variation.

A process behavior chart was developed in 1924 by Walter Shewhart and taught to the world by W. Edwards Deming to detect the difference between these systemic and special causes of variation; unfortunately, most of the world has not accepted this profound knowledge as a means of attaining effective leadership. This lack of knowledge creates immeasurable loss in terms of profits, worker income, and gross domestic product.

Let me suggest a golf analogy to illustrate these two kinds of variation. Suppose that on one green, you putt the ball past the hole, but then on the next green, you consciously or unconsciously tamper with and adjust your golf swing, which causes overcompensation, which means you frequently putt the ball short of the hole. The same condition applies when shooting an arrow with a bow; if you miss the target by several inches to the right, it would seem logical that you would just aim several inches to the left to hit the center, but you would be wrong most of the time.

In both instances, if you do not determine whether the problem is a special cause (unpredictable) or a systemic cause of variation (predictable within limits), you will be prone to tamper and overcompensate. An understanding of these two types of variation will improve the accuracy of your putting swing and the aim of each arrow so that your golf and archery scores will improve.

Eighty-five to 95 percent of the causes of defects, problems, and harmful or undesirable results within any organization—and indeed a nation—are systemic. The world has it backward, because organizations and nations respond to 85 to 95 percent of the errors and problems as special causes. The lack of understanding of these two types of variation creates a very blaming and judgmental society—that is, we blame individuals for systemic causes of variation that are beyond their control and often their ability to understand. Every worker can relate to being blamed for results that were out of his or her control.

The following are some systemic causes of variation: corporate culture; unrealistic goals; confusing and complicated processes; lack of training; performance appraisals that create internal competition; pay for meeting performance goals; lack of clear operational definitions of expectations and terms. When we blame and judge individuals for systemic causes of variation—meaning, tasks and processes that are out of their complete control—we are showing them unkindness and a lack of compassion. An understanding of variation of phenomena and its underlying causes has everything to do with our ability to show empathy and compassion; therefore, it is in the realm of spiritual awareness and spirituality.

After several years of research into the mysteries of life and the spiritual laws/principles of the universe, I realized the valuable and beneficial implications of my revelation, which was followed by an instant understanding of variation as it applies to these mysteries of life and spiritual principles. This one and only realization in my life, which I assumed at the time was only about increasing my technical knowledge, was *instrumental several years later in my discovery of the origin of ignorance and the meaning and purpose of creation*, and it has changed my way of thinking about life, God, others, and myself.

I had this realization when I was looking at an overhead screen while narrating a presentation. A realization is different from learning, insight, or even a discovery. One's realization cannot be shared with anyone else. Only the knowledge of one's realization can be shared. It occurs in the moment and removes all doubts. After your realization, there is no defensive behavior when others attack you or reject your new understanding, because there are no doubts to defend.

It is impossible to return to your previous mode of being and thinking in the world after a realization has occurred. Doing so would be like asking oneself to believe that two plus two is five. A realization is not a conversion, as a conversion is based on accepting a certain set of beliefs, whereas a realization gives the person a new clarity of awareness about a certain reality.

A realization follows a revelation. A revelation is a surprise or an awakening, whereas a realization is a new understanding or awareness. They occur almost simultaneously. There was no deep-seated emotional response, just a slight smile accompanied by a knowing beyond knowing that I had never experienced previously. I saw a new aspect of life as it applied to the relative-phenomenal world with such clarity that I am unable explain the feeling to this day.

In that one moment when I realized that variation was the key to successful leadership in an organization, a knowing beyond knowing awareness came into my consciousness. I knew that knowledge of variation was the key to continual improvement and successful leadership, because we live in a world of variety and phenomena.

Stated another way, variation has to do with the relative part of this world, whereas phenomena have to do with the temporal and transient individualized aspects of this world in the realm of serial experiences. As stated earlier, for you and me to have a perceived separate identity, to interact with each other and to have a relationship with each other, there must be a perception of a difference (variation) between us. Likewise, for you and me to have experiences, there must be a perception of observable phenomena.

The variation of phenomena is the very core of our life experiences. It is through these experiences in the human realm that our souls have the opportunity to awaken to our spirits within and acquire intelligence. The variation of phenomena is also the process whereby this Oneness (God) expresses itself in an infinite variety of expressions. All of creation is relative; thus, all of creation has variation. Indeed, the very necessity of creation is variation, for without differences there is only the stillness of Pure Awareness.

If a sincere seeker can understand why all of creation out of necessity is relative, then that person will be better able to attain knowledge of the origin of suffering, the origin of ignorance, and the meaning and purpose of life. Only God is not relative (meaning without variation), and it is the necessity of Oneness to create, because God is a dynamic God, not a God of infinite stillness.

A dynamic reality demands a relative-phenomenal world. The very act of creation creates a conscious reality, which is always relative and with phenomena that are temporal and transient.

Variation and phenomena are the foundation of human life. What we see and experience is the drama of life. Those who teach that life is but an illusion fail to see that we are living souls, and as such, we are the dynamic reality of this infinite vitality and divine intelligence expressing its unlimited potential. The illusion is that we feel separate from this Infinite Oneness. This illusion has meaning and purpose, for it is a necessity for Oneness to be more than just the absolute stillness of Perfect Awareness, but a dynamic and creative God. We as living souls are examples of the nature of God.

There can never be two absolute realities within one Infinite Oneness. It is a necessity for Oneness to appear as multiplicity (variation), so there must be a perception of other. The entire universe is Oneness. In fact, there is no space. What we perceive as space is actually a false perception. Absolutely everything in this universe is made up of energy (vitality), including our bodies. There is no such thing as empty space.

The same energy that makes up our flesh and bones is the same energy that makes up the building or house you are now sitting in. This flesh and bone is made up of trillions of cells, which are in turn made up of what's called organelles (little organs). Each of these organelles performs a different function. For example, the mitochondria are organelles that are considered the cell's power source because they generate most of its energy.

Hence, if we are made up of energy, and if every possible space around us is energy, then aren't we connected to one another? And if we are all connected to one another (oneness), doesn't that also mean that we are connected to an Infinite Source, or God? When I set out on this journey, I suspected I might find that God was a fabrication of our imagination because of our fear of death. Remember, I was practically an atheist or an agnostic, and I leaned toward materialism as the stuff of life. Instead, I found that believing in a God with human traits is a fabrication of our ego.

To my surprise, I discovered a source that I shall call Supreme or Divine Awareness that is centered in love, has perfect intelligence, and that creates infinite uniqueness. What is so amazing is that every soul, every human, every plant, every tree, and every snowflake is unique. The Infinite Source of all creation does not duplicate its creation.

Before I go any further, I must point out that I have no idea where this profound understanding of variation in this relative-phenomenal world came from. One minute I was teaching a seminar, and the next, I had instant knowledge in the form of understanding. Having an understanding about something is far different from intellectual knowledge. Understanding is a knowing beyond knowing that is not based in beliefs. One can always tell whether a person has an understanding or a belief by the way he or she acts. Defensive behavior stems from beliefs that harbor doubt; meekness is a demonstration of understanding.

We can change beliefs, but not understanding. "The meek shall inherit the earth" now has a different meaning for me, as meekness is about understanding, not just beliefs.

Understanding is eternal. It is a knowing beyond knowing. Most of what we know is intellectual knowledge that we confuse for understanding, and it causes us many problems. Only when we experience the realization of a truth do we realize the significance of understanding. A realization is with our soul for the duration of our journey toward Oneness. When we are able to view this world's experience through our soul eyes, we realize that we are seeking to acquire intelligence as a soul. Understanding is intelligence, not intellectualism.

When we have something of divine value, it is intrinsic to our soul, and we have acquired this understanding for eternity. Our understanding is now a truth without doubts. We have realized a universal truth. Over time, we see the ramifications of our understanding, and we learn how it can apply to our world, our universe, and even our perception of God. Realization is beyond beliefs, faith, conversion, insights, or discovery. A revelation that causes a realization changes our lives because we see the world anew.

As I said above, revelations change how we view everything about our lives, including God. In my case, I made many discoveries about God and the universe, but I wondered about many things too: If God is love, why is there so much suffering in the world? If suffering is the culprit of ignorance, as the Buddha and many others have taught, then what is the origin of that ignorance? If God is love and love is bliss, why would bliss have a need or necessity to create anything less than perfection?

At first, I thought that understanding variation was simply the key to effective leadership within an organization. I soon realized the profound implications of having understanding of the variation within a relative world and later the divine discovery of how an understanding of variation applied to innocence and the creation of conscious souls capable of seeing other souls as different.

To my amazement, my revelation/realization on variation led me to understand that in order to live in a relative-phenomenal world we must be unaware of our true nature, which is spirit. Spirit is the very essence of all souls.

I truly believe that the most interesting topic we can discuss or write about is God. This God, or what I like to call the Pure Awareness of Divine Intelligence, has been a mystery to everyone but the mystics, who see the reality of the oneness of the universe. (We will discuss Divine Intelligence in the next chapter.) When they try to explain their philosophy to us, however, we often turn a deaf ear because we are unable to understand their view of reality.

As you read this book, think of God as the source of all things seen and unseen. I sometimes use the terms Perfect Love/Intelligence and Christ Consciousness rather than God. This word, it seems to me, has many different connotations and nuances. Humankind has given God human traits and qualities, and this causes us to miss the divine meaning of many words, such as love and intelligence.

It is a necessity for God to express Itself. This Oneness of all that is or ever will be must create entities (souls) with less than perfect awareness and intelligence, because to do otherwise would be the duplication of its Infinite Awareness, not the creation of unique souls. Our limited awareness is what makes us unique. What is uniqueness but differences? Again, Oneness cannot duplicate itself because it is infinite, and you cannot have two infinites.

What Oneness does is initiate an evolution-of-consciousness process that creates entities that have less than perfect awareness or intelligence. This creates the perception of "otherness" because we lack perfect intelligence and the power to see ourselves as Oneness. This is why at this lower phase of soul development we harm one another. We don't yet have the intelligence or understanding to know that when we harm one another, we are actually harming ourselves, because we are all one with God. Because of this Oneness, whatever we do to others, we do to ourselves. With our limited intelligence, we perceive ourselves as separate humans and souls. Like children, we err because we have less than perfect intelligence or awareness.

Those errors that most call sin are based in this created lack of intelligence. Our lack of perfect intelligence is defined as ignorance or unawareness. All sin, all error, and all evil have at their very core some degrees of unawareness.

Where indeed does this ignorance come from? It comes from the Creator/God. This Source of all creation created us with less than perfect intelligence so that Oneness can become innumerable *beings*, and so that, in a remarkable and mysterious way, this Oneness can have a relationship with and interact with *Itself*. How could Oneness have a relationship with Itself if it is Oneness? Two or more beings that perceive themselves as separate personalities must have a relationship in order to interact. Involution, the process of Oneness becoming many, allows Oneness to have a perception of others.

Again, if Josie and I had perfect intelligence, there would be no ability to express our unique differences. God is expressing its dynamic potential and literally experiencing itself through every unique soul ever created. This involution process we call creation has an infinite variation of potential and expressions.

In other words, through the process of evolution, our souls grow and evolve toward God and some believe back to God or Perfect Awareness. Involution is just the opposite, as this process creates less than perfect souls that are innocent of their true identities, which is God. This allows us to experience life as perceived separate beings that most call souls.

The spirit within each soul provides it with vitality and intelligence, but out of necessity, each soul has been created with limited intelligence. This creative involution process exists to give each soul a perception of being unique and therefore separate from all other souls.

Limited or less than perfect intelligence is unawareness or ignorance defined. If there were no imperfections in creation (meaning limited awareness, not mistakes or errors), nothing would differentiate it from the Creator. As Emmanuel stated, "What you are is perfect imperfection" (*Emmanuel's Book One*).

Pretend for a moment that you are God and you want to express yourself in an infinite number of ways. Remember, you are All in All; you are Infinite. You have Perfect Awareness, and you know everything there is to know about everything. You have unlimited vitality and power. You are Oneness and feel a necessity to share your awareness with others. What would you do and how would you do it?

Remember, you are all that is. So would you create a universe of entities exactly like yourself? Would you use a cookie-cutter approach and create entities that were alike but ignorant? How would you create each soul different from every other soul you have ever created? What process would you use to create uniqueness?

If we are all created perfect, then we can't all be unique. So would you then decide to make souls imperfect or ignorant? These imperfections and our experiences, indeed our struggles, mold us over time into unique souls with infinite potential. Most who have lived a long life know that it has been their struggles, difficulties, problems, and even suffering that have taught them the most about compassion, which is simply love in action. We are all perfectly imperfect for a divine reason. The closer we get to perfection and perfect awareness, the closer we get to God.

As Jesus stated, "Be ye therefore perfect, even as your Father which is in heaven is perfect" (Matthew 5:48 KJV Bible). These were not idle words spoken by Jesus, but accurate statements about the reality of our journey. Intelligence is inspired spiritual wisdom. Inspiration for perfection comes from God through the spirit within us.

When the sages and mystics tell us we are asleep, it is their way of telling us that we do not see reality, or, stated another way, the underlying reality of phenomena. They are correct in that we fail to realize the full extent of our divine reality. We are ignorant, meaning unaware of our divinity. Anthony de Mello, a Jesuit priest, writes in his book *One Minute Wisdom*, "Wisdom tends to grow in proportion to one's awareness of one's ignorance."

Perfect Love manifests a facet of its nature through spirit. Perfect Intelligence manifests and creates innocent souls to express itself as unique identities in the astral and physical worlds. Only through innocence can God manifest its dynamic potential as unique identities in the astral and physical worlds. Only through innocence can God manifest itself as separate identities that can demonstrate love and intelligence to one another. Oneness becomes infinite identities through the process of creation of innocent souls.

It is as simple as this: if no original innocence, then no separate expressions of God's oneness. Of course, what is often simple to state can be profoundly difficult to understand. For example, "love your enemies" is very easy to say, but it is profoundly difficult to understand or even have a minimum knowledge of its divine implications.

We sin when we condemn others or ourselves because we are in error of our reality. We spend all of our incarnations eating from the tree of knowledge. Knowledge becomes divine intelligence when we attain these inner realizations. Knowing the difference between knowledge and intelligence changes our beliefs as to our reality. Knowledge does not give us understanding or realization. That must come through revelation, but it appears that knowledge and insights can be a precursor to a realization.

Remember, we awaken in degrees of understanding, but as each revelation occurs, it moves us ever closer to realizing that we are the essence of God's love. We must acquire divine intelligence through the realization of a truth. We do not acquire love; we are love. The very essence of our soul is love.

Before a revelation occurs, there is usually a long period of seeking for most aspirants, but not always. Why some seek their whole lives and have no revelations and others only seek for years and the divine wisdom of a truth is revealed to them is due to the multitude of variables inherent in a revelation. An aspirant's past karma and level of soul development are two of the significant variables that determine the timing and likelihood of a revelation. Perfection, like karma, shows no favoritism.

DIVINE INTELLIGENCE

"All great truths begin as blasphemies."
—George Bernard Shaw

Saint Paul had a blind revelation on the road to Damascus and said, "Let this mind be in you, which was also in Christ Jesus" (Philippians 2:5, KJV Bible) He also stated, "The creation waits in eager expectation for the sons of God to be revealed" (Romans 8:19, New International Version). Was Paul suggesting Christ Consciousness for all of us? It certainly appears that way by his suggestion that we humans, as sons of God, let the likeness of Jesus's mind be in all humankind.

Saint Paul did not achieve perfect intelligence with his revelation. Many of the statements attributed to him in the New Testament suggest that his religious and cultural beliefs still influenced his views of reality. Isn't it interesting that a Pharisee who once persecuted Christians became the person who many believe saved the Christian religion from extinction?

As Jesus stated in one of his teachings, we need to be perfect as the Father in heaven is perfect. It is evident that He understood soul evolution as the process we humans use to attain this perfection. Through this process, we awaken to our perfect spirit within, and through revelation, we acquire divine intelligence. As we attain this divine intelligence, we become more like that which is the Source of all creation. Most refer to this source as God.

If God is perfect, then anything that is not perfect is temporal reality or phenomena. We realize why the Eastern mystics call this temporal earth experience *Maya* (illusion). The infinite us is not our bodies, our egos, or our souls, but our spirits. The eternal us is our soul. Our souls are in progress, whereas our spirits are a spark of God. An understanding of soul evolution by more of the earth's human population will have a significant and influential impact on our progress as a planet, because such an understanding will compel us to live together in love and intelligence.

The interesting thing is that we believe everyone else hides from truth, but we fail to see how we hide from truth and how our beliefs control our view of reality. Ask an avowed atheist if he thinks religious people allow beliefs to influence their views of reality. His answer will usually be, "Absolutely," and he will probably tell you more on this subject than you want to hear. Then ask that same atheist if his beliefs influence his ability to see reality, and listen to how he responds to that question. Very few realize how much the conviction of our beliefs influences our view of reality.

The stuff of life and consciousness is thoughts. We are conscious beings because we have thoughts. Each of us has unique thoughts, which is what makes us unique. Without thoughts, there is no us—only Isness or Oneness. When the Infinite Mind (God) had a thought or thoughts, the universe was created. The universe, which has the appearance of matter, is consciousness. As our thoughts advance in awareness, love and divine intelligence become our mode of being in the world.

The *essence* of spirit is awareness. Awareness is the understanding of reality. We are souls on a journey of becoming more self-aware as being a manifestation of God (Infinite Awareness). All manifestation occurs by creating consciousness. The more aware of reality those thoughts become, the more they are in alignment with this Infinite Mind. As consciousness grows, our awareness expands in infinite love and divine intelligence.

When we state that God is love, this is not quite correct. The statement that God is love is a statement *about* God, not a statement about what God *is* or *is not*. God cannot be defined because infinite cannot be perfectly defined. As I mentioned earlier in this book, to define infinite is to limit the concept of infinite. What we can do, however, is make a statement about the attributes of Infinite Awareness with our limited awareness. "God is love" is a wonderful statement about an attribute of God, which is Infinite Love. The more aware we become of ourselves as expressions of God, the more we are able to love others and ourselves. How awe-inspiring is it to be an expression of Infinite Love?

Our intelligence comes from this unbounded and limitless Divine Mind. Just as God had a thought that created the universe of consciousness, we have thoughts that create our realities. The more divine our thoughts, the more loving and intelligent our reality. Heaven is having a loving and intelligent flow of thoughts that create a loving and beautiful mode of existence in this world or other worlds. Heaven, like all dimensions we reside in, is our level of thoughts and the awareness of reality within those thoughts.

Consciousness is all around us, as it is a conscious universe. The thought or thoughts of God are consciousness. Most scientists are baffled by the concept of consciousness. Those who believe that the brain is the center of consciousness have to deal with a multitude of unanswered questions. For instance, how do some children speak a foreign language at an early age without any prior family history or knowledge of it?

Xenoglossia, which is an unexplainable use of a foreign language, is considered one of many evidences of reincarnation. (We will discuss reincarnation in further detail in the next chapter.) Some insist on explaining away consciousness as a brain function without even considering the evidence of metaphysical and paranormal activity. Research into physical phenomena will leave most in wonder of the over-whelming evidence for an astral realm of existence for us all. Those who say that statements about an astral world are just wishful thinking demonstrate their lack of perseverance in doing unbiased research.

Aside from this consciousness, it is love that makes up this experience we call life. Some form of love and intelligence connects everything that we know as matter and space. What is space? It is not emptiness, but love manifested in many unique forms and phenomena. We humans have only touched the surface of our ability to love self and others. As souls that have perceptions of self, we are in the very early stages of our development in divine love and intelligence.

We have no idea how many dimensions or worlds are in our future. Those who say there are seven levels or dimensions are saying what they believe, not what they could possibly know. Who among us can claim with certainty the number of dimensions our soul will reside in as it journeys toward the infinite?

We are all connected, as we are all in our very essence love. It is natural for us to seek to be more like the Infinite Source of all creation, and with time and experiences, to realize perfect love for others and ourselves. When Eve ate from the tree of the knowledge of good and evil, she was expressing an inner longing to be like her Creator with infinite love and divine intelligence.

We desire to be perfect love, but in our innocence, this soon reveals itself as ignorance, and often this ignorance leads to misguided desire. This is why we can state that all sin and evil is misguided desire, and of course, all misguided desire has its origin in our ignorance of our perfect reality, which is Spirit.

A truism to live by is that all sin and evil is an effect, not a cause. The causal reality of all sin and evil is ignorance, and the underlying reality of all ignorance is our original innocence. This aspect of sin and evil is extremely difficult to comprehend and accept because we judge by appearances.

The more advanced a soul becomes in divine intelligence; the more advanced the viewpoint of the self and the world. When we are egotistical, we are demonstrating an unaware mode of being in the world or worlds. As developing souls, we must pass through an egotistical phase of existence in which we feel and act separately from others. This phase could be several lifetimes as a human in order for us to learn our lessons in life about love and divine intelligence.

No sage or enlightened human exists without having gone through an egotistical, self-centered phase of soul development. The purpose of this phase is to create a perceived separate identity. We learn the lessons of this phase of development year-by-year, day by day, and moment by moment. This is why advanced spirits are so compassionate. They have lived through their own egotistical phase and understand their meaning and purpose. They would not be where they are today in their understanding without having lived through the harshness of their human experiences, which has helped them to advance in awareness on their journey toward Infinite Oneness. God does not express its dynamic potential without this journey of many souls.

KARMA AND REINCARNATION

"My karma ran over your dogma."

—Bumper sticker

Webster's Dictionary defines *karma* as the total effect of a person's actions and conduct during the successive phases of existence, held to determine destiny in Hinduism and Buddhism. In other words, karma implies that we are all reaping what we have sown in previous lives, and we are sowing what we will reap in another life. It is the law of cause and effect.

As a cosmic mirror, karma does not play favorites. It is a law or principle that applies to individuals, nations, and the entire universe. Obviously, for any of this to be true, reincarnation must also be true.

Reincarnation makes the case that the body is just a cloak used by our soul when it comes to earth to experience life, to learn lessons, and to advance in spiritual awareness. Some take comfort in reincarnation and see it as a divine plan, but to others, it represents a grotesque cycle because the soul is constantly held accountable for its actions. To me it doesn't matter what stance you take. The real question is whether reincarnation is real.

The ancient Egyptians built their beliefs on reincarnation and karma. Eastern cultures teach reincarnation as a natural part of life. They consider those of us who don't believe in it to be spiritually blind, because to them it is no-brainer. Yet many continue to seek proof.

While it is correct to say that reincarnation has not been scientifically proven, there are many so-called arguments for reincarnation, including, among others, past life memories among children, moments of déjà vu, and Xenoglossia.

One of the most recent cases for reincarnation involves the story of a little boy named James Leininger, who was obsessed with playing with airplanes at a very young age. When he turned two, he began to have nightmares during which he would say things like, "Airplane crash on fire, little man can't get out!"

His parents didn't know what to believe as their son continued to show clear signs that he was remembering a past life. James told his parents that he had flown a Corsair that was hit by the Japanese and crashed at Iwo Jima. He gave them specific details about the plane, the name of another pilot, the name of the ship his plane took off from, and more.

Research later revealed that everything James was saying was correct. During World War II, there was a pilot named James M. Huston Jr. who served aboard the *Natoma Bay*. Huston was killed when the Corsair he was flying was struck during a raid near Iwo Jima. This incredible story is one of many in which people have recollections of past lives.

Do stories like these prove that reincarnation is real? I think it's a personal matter. What constitutes proof for one person may carry absolutely no weight for someone else. Some people wonder why all humans cannot remember their previous lives. That is certainly a valid question. An equally valid response would be that just because we don't remember something doesn't mean that we never lived it. You lived the first year of your life, but you don't remember anything about it. Does that mean you were never here? Of course, it doesn't.

Keep in mind, though, that God is not in the business of messing up. Perfect Awareness has perfect understanding.

Every soul is unique and no accident. The infinite experiences we have and the choices we make are what we live and learn from. We are all in this together, thus the concept of Oneness. The belief that we are separate from others causes a soul to feel alone and fearful in the world, and many problems arise. The role of karma, then, is to give us feedback so that we can learn from the fruits of love and divine intelligence.

Paul Brunton (1898–1981), an accomplished philosopher and author, wrote, "Every act is reflected back to the doer, and every thought is reflected back to the source like a vast cosmic mirror." Brunton termed this the law of reflection.

All of these universal or divine laws are based on the reality that all is Oneness. We are expressions of this Oneness, and whatever we do to others, we do to ourselves. In our selfishness, we think we can cheat these universal laws, but it is impossible. Oneness is everything, and nothing can deceive the universal principle of Oneness. To harm another is to harm self. To judge another is to judge self. We are in the midst of a learning process of insights, discoveries, and realizations combined with karma as a reflection of our actions and thoughts, which come back to us so that we can become more loving and compassionate.

Again, we are all souls on a journey, and the major part of this journey is to learn and in time realize that we are connected to the Source, which is Oneness. Life on earth as a soul is akin to a nursery school where souls come to learn lessons and advance in love and intelligence. It is wise to keep in mind that the best is yet to come, but we must also keep our eyes focused on the present, because it offers the best opportunities for soul growth and development.

SUMMARY

"Perfection is attained by slow degrees; it requires the hand of time."

—Voltaire

God, which is Infinite, cannot be perfectly defined, for to define infinite is to limit infinite. We can only dance around the definition of God with words such as Pure and Perfect Awareness, Infinite Awareness, Divine Love, Infinite Love, Infinite Intelligence, Divine Intelligence, That That Is, All in All, Absolute, or Isness.

There are two aspects to God: stillness and dynamic potential. The great German mystic Meister Eckhart called this stillness the Godhead, and this Godhead, to Eckhart, was like the stillness of a barren desert. Then there is the vibrant, pulsating, and creative side to God, and we as living souls, with our limited but ever increasing awareness of reality, are living proofs of the vitality and energetic expressions of God.

This aspect of the dynamic vitality of God makes it a necessity for God to create its infinite and ongoing becomingness and never-ending potential. God does this by creating unique souls, as every soul expresses this infinite vitality of God as a unique *manifestation* of God. A synonym for manifestation is expression. This variation in levels of consciousness reveals itself as a relative-phenomenal world of dimensions, as all of creation is relative.

God's necessity to express its dynamic self and infinite potential requires the creation of eternal souls. The variation of each soul's uniqueness is an expression of God, which allows each soul to perceive it and others as different.

This soul variation is accomplished through the evo-lution-of-consciousness process. To experience another requires consciousness that sees variation of phenomena; hence a relative-phenomenal reality for eternal souls. The perception of a relative-phenomenal reality requires souls to be innocent of their intrinsic reality (spirit), and this innocence manifests itself as ignorance once a soul starts its journey to acquire intelligence.

Ignorance leads to error because a soul has not *yet* acquired that which is available to be known. This error is often labeled *sin* by those who lack knowledge or understanding of God's necessity to express its potential in an infinite number of individualized manifestations. These unique expressions of God that we call souls have limited awareness, and this is for a very profound reason. God expresses its potential, indeed its infinite potential, in an infinite variety of unique souls as divine expressions of its Self as Infinite Oneness.

The reality is that every soul is created unique, and thus variation exists because of each soul's limited awareness. We as souls are not responsible for our unique, limited awareness. We as souls did not create the creation process that made us unique and with limited but increasing awareness. The ability of God to create an infinite number of unique souls is so mind boggling that it cannot be fathomed.

The original root meaning of the word responsibility was *the ability to respond.* The term personal responsibility has been profoundly misinterpreted and therefore misused to suggest that we are culpable and blameworthy. We as souls are divine expressions created with original unawareness, without which there is no expression of That That Is. The religious and atheists alike deny this aspect of our unawareness. The unaware ego prefers culpability and blameworthiness; this allows an ego to judge others as inferior to itself.

The ego is very deceptive in its misguided desire to feel guilt and take personal responsibility for its sins due to its limited awareness. Guilt is the ego's almost infinite ability to deceive, and this is based in fear. To feel separate from all others is the underlying reason for an ego's need for guilt, culpability, and self-blame. This is individualism defined.

Individualism is often just a hidden and accepted term for selfishness and self-centered behavior. An important truism: uniqueness is the creation of God, and individualism is of human origin to feel and act separately from all others.

Our *original innocence* is that we as souls did not create or design the evolution-of-consciousness process. This process has created each soul in the universe as a unique soul with limited but boundless awareness. No two souls are alike in their awareness.

Newer souls with less awareness make more errors than older, mature souls, and we humans call these errors sins. In our created unawareness, we often label these souls on a human journey as evil, but we do so in our ignorance. Evil and sin have their home in ignorance, which is our limited awareness.

The creation process that creates each soul unique can be called the involution process, which we view as the creation aspect of God. This process creating of unique and distinctive souls takes place on a continual basis. When we view responsibility as the ability to respond, this opens our minds to see with greater clarity our original innocence and the fact that we are always innocent in the mind of God.

We cannot take responsibility for our created original innocence. We as souls desperately want to take responsibility for our mistakes and the choices we make; this gives us a sense of having a separate personal identity. Without realizing it, this causes us to feel separate from God and all others. Our greatest fear is losing our personal and cherished identity in a sea of nothingness.

Quite frankly, we humans would rather be called sinners and experience guilt than be called or thought of as ignorant, not realizing that ignorance is nothing more than our created original innocence due to our limited awareness of our godliness. As Dr. Hora taught so correctly, guilt is one of the most devious self-confirmatory modes of being in the world, as it leaves God out of our lives as our creator. We are not separate from God but expressions of God. We live, move, and have our being within the infinite mind of God. Therefore, separateness is impossible and unattainable no matter how hard the ego endeavors to be a separate entity out of fear of losing its very fragile identity.

That original innocence, created by an involution-of-awareness process, reveals itself to others and to the world as *ignorance*. A synonym for limited awareness or unawareness is ignorance. With limited awareness, a soul will err in its choices, which most call free will. Free will is a fallacy that has been taught by society and religion. However, if we define free will as having limitations, then indeed we do have free will to make choices, but within boundaries. Those boundaries are our limited awareness or our degrees of unawareness.

With our limited awareness, we cannot make perfect choices or live perfect lives, contrary to what this world and even some spirit beings that reside in other worlds teach us. Nevertheless, there is hope, because as our awareness expands, we express greater levels of Divine Love and Infinite Intelligence. Thus, we are unique expressions of God.

God does not create every soul perfect. Adam and Eve were not created with perfect awareness but were innocent. Most in the world, with their limited awareness, have failed to see this aspect of the biblical story. Only when Adam and Eve ate from the tree of the knowledge of good and evil, which is the evolution-of-consciousness learning process for all souls, did they know death and suffering. The Garden of Eden was a paradise of innocence, not perfect awareness.

This evolution-of-consciousness process is called *evolution*. Involution is the process from Oneness to many souls, and evolution puts each soul on a unique "only one of its kind journey". This journey of the soul is the dynamic aspect of God and indeed is the necessity of God to express its infinite potential.

Both involution and evolution are the creative aspects of God, which we cannot fully comprehend. The involution process is the unfolding of *God's* infinite potential; the evolution process, with its almost infinite experiences, is creating every soul unique and with almost unlimited potential. There is one limit to a soul's potential. The only limit and boundary is that a soul cannot exist outside of or separate from Infinite Oneness. Of course, as a soul journeys through its expansion-of-consciousness process, it is God expressing its potential in an infinite number of manifestations and unique expressions.

Those who have had a near-death experience (NDE) or other spiritual occurrences often end up with a huge expansion in awareness. This vast expansion in awareness is called by most a mystical experience. Those who have had this mystical NDE experience have come back with similar knowledge of this Infinite Love. Many call this experience a hallucination, but only in their innocence.

The necessity of Infinite Awareness is to create and express its dynamic potential in an infinite variation of expressions, which are manifestations of God. This is accomplished by each soul being created with a spark of awareness that expands with serial experiences, which create time and karma. This is the law of progress defined. If God created every soul with infinite and perfect awareness, there would be no *us*, just *Isness*. Duplication of infinite is impossible, but not uniqueness. The oneness of God becomes many souls through the manifestation process of our original innocence.

Listed below is the sequence of events that the soul goes through during the processes of involution and evolution:

Creation: from the stillness of perfect awareness to the dynamic potential of God

Manifestation: creation from the infinite Oneness of God

Innocence: a necessity for the creation of unique souls

Ignorance: the world's view of innocence

Suffering: every soul's unaware choices, caused by ignorance

Karma: what we sow, we reap, with an opportunity for a new awareness of reality

In this book, we have described the three mysteries of life:

The origin of our suffering: Why do we suffer so?

The origin of our ignorance: Why are we not created perfect?

The meaning of creation: God expresses its love and divine intelligence as infinite souls.

The Answers:

The origin of our suffering is ignorance: our created limited awareness.

The origin of our ignorance is innocence: the involution process, from oneness to many.

The meaning of creation is evident in souls, which are the divine and dynamic expressions of God. The evolution-of-the-soul process is the evolution-of-consciousness process. God makes itself known through the creation of unique souls.

The reality of creation is that we as souls cannot take responsibility for our ignorance. We as humans desperately want to, but we err in this misguided desire. This desire, however, is only due to our limited awareness. We did not create the process that created us with our limited awareness.

It is this inner awareness or spirit within us that guides us, but we can be overcome with misguided desires when we judge by appearances, which is our limited awareness in action, but we did not create this limited awareness, we cannot take responsibility for it. We are responsible for the choices we make on our evolutionary journey. This might seem like a paradox, but it isn't. We cannot take responsibility for our limited awareness, but we are responsible for and affected by our choices. We are responsible because every choice has a cause-and-effect outcome to teach us the profound lessons of life.

Just because we were created with original innocence does not mean that we do not suffer the consequences of our actions. "What we sow, we reap" was one of the most profound lessons ever taught by Jesus. Many call this karma. Most mystics I have studied and the spirits that reside in higher dimensions or spheres have stated that their struggles and suffering from their misguided actions were crucial aspects of their awakening.

Without karma, there would be no evolution of consciousness of the soul, and it is this evolution, along with time and experiences, that makes every soul unique. This uniqueness of each soul expresses the dynamic potential of God's infinite intelligence and vitality. The journey of the soul is from a spark of awareness to a divine expression of God. This law of karma is a divine principle or law—not punishment, as most teach, but it sure can feel like it, and often it has the appearance of punishment.

Does it not make perfect sense that God always sees its creation as innocent? Perfect love sees our innocence, which is the underlying reality of all phenomena. To even suggest that perfect love would demand any type of atonement is heresy in the highest order, but only out of unawareness would anyone suggest such an idea.

Love sees innocence, and when we have this understanding, which is a knowing beyond knowing, we are able to discern the underlying reality of our perceived errors as innocence. This is what the spirit being in the light gray gown revealed to me during my life review that felt to me as perfect love and compassion. Once you experience that love and compassion, you never forget it.

When Jesus stated on the cross, "Forgive them, for they know not what they do," he had understanding of our innocence, and that was a profound and divine teaching moment. The Buddha saw the origin of our suffering as our ignorance, whereas Jesus saw the origin of our ignorance/unawareness as our innocence. Interesting to note that most Buddhists, even most Buddhist monks, lack knowledge of what the Buddha realized, and they confuse symptoms with origins. Symptoms of ignorance are attachment, craving, grasping, and so on.

The world is suffering from ignorance, but we are always innocent in the "eyes" of God, contrary to what most of the world's religions teach. The underlying reality and origin of that ignorance is innocence. The following is what I call a visualization diagram to help readers understand the connection between the Godhead and our suffering:

Godhead
Infinite Love and Divine Intelligence

Creation
Vitality and substance to living forms
Expression of God's infinite potential

Manifestation
From Oneness to many souls

Innocence
The evolution-of-consciousness process
The necessity for the creation of unique souls

Ignorance
To imperfect eyes, innocence becomes ignorance

Suffering
For you shall be as gods knowing good from evil.
Therefore,
The origin of our suffering is ignorance.
The origin of our ignorance is innocence.
The origin of our innocence is manifestation.
The origin of manifestation is the creation process.
The creation process is the Godhead's infinite potential.

QUESTIONS AND ANSWERS: THE THREE MYSTERIES OF LIFE

"The important thing is not to stop questioning. Curiosity has its own reason for existing."

—Albert Einstein

My premise during my years of research into seeking truth was that *perfection cannot create imperfection unless it desires to do so.* Perfection does not make mistakes. Believing that Perfection (God) gave humans free will to spend eternity in hell makes a travesty of God's divine intelligence.

Logic and reasoning should tell us otherwise, but logic and reasoning are not always the best of human traits, especially when they challenge our conditioned and cherished beliefs. We cannot say in one breath that God knows all and is perfect love, then say in the next breath that God gave to every soul the opportunity to spend eternity in hell. This would mean that a fragment of God (spirit) within all of us would be in hell for eternity.

The belief that the devil tempts us with sin fails to acknowledge the relationship of evil and ignorance. I find that those who need a personal God with human traits also need a personal devil with undesirable human traits. It is easier to conceive of God with human traits and human form than a formless deity with perfect awareness.

This book shows us how looking through our soul's eyes helps us to move past beliefs and closer to reality. Because of my revelation on variation in a relative-phenomenal world, I was given the opportunity to attain the knowledge of the

69

correlation of creation/manifestation, variation/phenomena, innocence/ignorance, and joy/suffering. This revelation on variation and its relationship to ignorance, and later many insights and discoveries, caused me to begin an intensive research mode to seek knowledge about our reality as a conscious entity.

My discovery was that the soul's journey from innocence to perfect love/intelligence is an evolutionary journey. In order to understand this evolutionary journey, I sought answers to three of life's greatest mysteries:

*What is the origin of suffering?

*What is the origin of ignorance?

*What is the meaning of creation?

I have asked myself these and many other questions over the past twenty years. Josie Varga and I have had many candid discussions about my spiritual quest, which led to the inclusion of the following question-and-answer section in this book. As I said earlier in the introduction, Josie and I do not agree on everything but we do share a knowing that we are all eternal beings with a purpose. Some answers are intentionally repeated to emphasize a certain point of view.

1. WHY DO YOU BELIEVE WE SUFFER?

Three profound mysteries must be solved by humanity before knowledge can be fully attained about the meaning and purpose of life. Most people blame our suffering on the wrath of God, and they claim that this is because we have separated from God or disobeyed God, and thus we have fallen from grace. Even those who are called New Age claim that we have fallen asleep and that somehow we must find our way back to God. All of these beliefs fail to see the infinite perfection of God.

The universe exhibits perfect laws and principles, so the following question has been a great mystery to humankind: If the universe or God has perfect laws, then why is there so much suffering in the world? This is a legitimate question to ask and one that has caused much philosophical dialogue in the history of humankind.

We cannot in one breath state that God has created perfect laws and principles, such as karma, which is the idea that we reap what we sow, and then in the next breath state that God created souls that have disobeyed God and fallen after succumbing to evil. This belief does not pass the simplest of logic tests. Souls are created with limited awareness out of necessity; this limited awareness is the cause of our suffering.

We did not create ourselves; therefore, this is our original innocence. This reveals itself as ignorance because one's soul experiences life with the choices and feedback it receives from karma. Many choices create suffering, but many create joy. The combination of joy and suffering is the ongoing, continual process of soul development. Our suffering has much to teach us; it can literally bring us to our knees, after which we begin to seek a new direction to our lives.

Of course, there is always the case for free will and the problem of humans misusing their free will and choosing evil over God. Can we really believe that an infinite deity that knows all (past, present, and future) and has infinite intelligence could err and give free will to souls so that they can disobey God's laws and endure such suffering? I once heard a five-year-old challenge this logic. The child had not yet been conditioned to many of these illogical religious beliefs.

We suffer because of our lack of knowing. This lack of knowing can be defined as ignorance, and the source of this ignorance has its home in the creation of innocent souls. A soul's longing to acquire love and divine intelligence to complete itself comes from the spirit within each soul, and this longing requires a soul to demonstrate its ignorance. All souls have been created innocent of their perfection, and this creative process reveals itself as ignorance (unawareness); likewise, all souls, with their imperfections, make wrong choices and have misguided desires that most call sin and evil. The root cause of sin and evil is ignorance.

2. WHAT IS THE ORIGIN OF SUFFERING? IF GOD IS NOT ANGRY WITH US, WHY IS THERE SO MUCH MISERY AND SUFFERING IN THE WORLD?

The origin of suffering is ignorance. In our ignorance, we humans have created an abundance of myths as to the cause of our suffering, such as, "We have sinned against God, and therefore we have separated from God," or "We have fallen from the grace of God due to our sinful thoughts and actions." Because of these invalid beliefs, we blame and judge others and ourselves. The reality is that an Infinite Oneness could never separate from its creation.

In addition, a God of infinite love is, by its very definition, infinite grace. Some writers and even several self-proclaimed enlightened individuals state that we have fallen from the grace of God. They have failed to see the perfection of God's love. They believe we have fallen from the grace of God because of the struggles and suffering they see and experience in their daily lives. This is why it is advantageous for humanity to discover that the origin of suffering is ignorance. Believing that we have fallen from the grace of God means that we fail to see the value of the human journey and its almost infinite experiences that advance our eternal souls.

Humanity must ask these three profound questions (p70) on a planetary scale: If God is defined as love and perfection, then why do we experience so much human suffering? The multitude of beliefs that we have developed over these past millennia to explain this question do not stand up to logic or reasoning.

Some of those beliefs are that we have disobeyed God; we have separated from God; we have a God with human traits that rewards, punishes, and judges us; we have a God that adopts us if we believe that someone had to die for our sins. Others believe that we have fallen asleep. These beliefs fail to see the perfection that is necessary to be the Infinite Source of all the underlying reality of phenomena in the universe.

Most of these beliefs have come about because we see and experience so much suffering in our lives and in the world. When we judge by appearances, it appears that God is angry with us, and we suffer the consequences of that anger. For us humans to move beyond judging by appearances, we must become sincere spiritual seekers and ask the right questions.

The first of these three profound questions is what is the origin of our suffering? When we ask this question long enough and diligently seek the answer, we discover that Buddha realized the answer to this question over twenty-five hundred years ago. What he discovered was that ignorance is the underlying cause of all suffering.

It is important that readers of this book ask themselves the following question: If the Buddha realized twenty-five hundred years ago that the origin of suffering was ignorance, then why is most of the world oblivious to the Buddha's realization? The plot thickens even further because most Buddhists do not realize that the Buddha realized that the origin of suffering is ignorance. Most Buddhists will tell you that the origin of suffering is attachment, craving, and grasping, but those are only symptoms of ignorance and unawareness.

The fact that most people do not see the Buddha's realization shows the power of unawareness and its ability to pass on invalid beliefs. Most humans would rather be called sinners and even feel guilty and culpable for their sins than admit to their ignorance. These invalid beliefs condition us and make it nearly impossible to see any reality other than our conditioned beliefs. I must emphasize that if we think we have an open mind, we don't, and if we state we have an open mind, this absolutely, positively proves that we don't.

Because Oneness cannot create anything outside of itself, it must create a perception of another by creating souls innocent of their divine reality. *Souls created innocent of their divine reality and with less than perfect love and intelligence are our original innocence.* The sequence of events for the formation and journey of the soul is creation, manifestation, innocence, ignorance, joy/suffering, revelations/realizations, love, and divine intelligence.

The good news is that a soul has no choice but to seek divine intelligence and awaken toward perfect love because of the spirit within each soul. This awakening process is the journey of all souls and the unique expression of God.

Contrary to most religious beliefs, souls do not suffer forever in a place called hell. Each soul draws closer to God as it acquires divine intelligence and awakens to the spirit within its essence. A state of consciousness that the spiritualists call Hades is for those souls that have not worked out their own self-hate in their physical life or lives. Hades is not a place of eternal punishment, but a place that a soul works through its lack of love for itself and others. There are spiritual guides, healers, and teachers to help a soul in a Hades environment if that soul has the knowledge and humility to ask for help.

3. ARE YOU SAYING THAT IT IS A SOUL'S CHOICE TO BECOME HUMAN?

The human ego will try to convince you that it is special and that it was created separate from God. It may even convince you that humans are special and alone in the universe. Our souls make us very complex beings. Human consciousness is profoundly different from that of animals. Animals don't worship gods, create educational institutions, or seek ways to travel to other planets.

Those who say that humans are different because of an evolutionary process due to chance are following the path of materialism with its origin in Darwinism. There is far too much evidence for an underlying reality of physical phenomena. Einstein stated, "Our theories determine what we shall observe in our experiments." If we have materialistic theories, our experiments will reveal to us a materialistic and mechanical universe.

As a soul matures, it chooses when to take the human journey and how much adversity it wants to experience during its incarnation as a human. Adversity gives a soul more opportunities to advance in divine intelligence. The desire to take this journey is driven by the spirit within each soul. Desire is not the culprit of our suffering, as many Eastern religions teach; rather, it is misguided desire, which can be traced all the way back in time to the involution process when each soul was created innocent of his or her perfect reality.

All souls have as their ultimate destiny a longing for perfect love and divine intelligence. The fate that a mature soul plans for itself while in the astral world, with help, of course, from its spiritual guides, teachers, and elders, plays out during its human incarnation. This intended fate is designed to give the soul opportunities to acquire greater levels of love and intelligence.

A soul may choose to seek a difficult journey as a human because a challenging human life gives a soul greater opportunity and potential to acquire intelligence. Adversity offers opportunities for soul development. Some souls may decide to possess a human body to enjoy the pleasures of physical existence, while other souls may choose an easy life. Most mature souls seek a challenging life that has opportunities to advance the soul in intelligence and awaken to the spirit within. As a soul matures in these spheres of existence, it is often allowed to visit these higher dimensions and receive a snapshot of what life is like within them. This gives them the courage and longing to seek greater levels of love and divine intelligence.

4. WHAT IS THE ORIGIN OF IGNORANCE?

When we accept the reality that the Buddha realized that the origin of suffering is ignorance, then the next valid and important question becomes: what is the origin of this ignorance? It is important for us to ask this question because ignorance causes so much suffering in our personal lives and in the world. Human suffering reveals our ignorance, and who among us is sincerely interested in remaining ignorant?

Without innocence, there is no creation. Without innocence, there is no ignorance or unawareness. Perfection is Oneness, so variation requires the innocence of our created unawareness. For us to see one another as separate entities demands our innocence of our reality, and for the perfection of God to create a consciousness of otherness demands innocence. Perfection is beyond our grasp at this time in our human and soul journey.

Jesus showed his divine intelligence when he made this statement about the spirit within him: "Believest thou not that I am in the Father, and the Father in me? The words that I speak unto you I speak not of myself: but the Father that dwelleth in me, he doeth the works" (John 14:10, KJV Bible).

This opened the door for religion to pronounce Jesus as God. He went on to say that "the kingdom of God is within you" (Luke 17:21, KJV Bible), but new editions of the Bible have revised this verse to read, "The kingdom of God is within your midst" (New American Standard Bible) and, "The kingdom of God is among you" (New Living Translation). These changes suggest that Jesus is not just a god but the only God.

At least this is what some disciples of a certain religion that showed up at my door one day were advocating to me when I asked why they believed that Jesus is God. These changes in translation were not done maliciously, but those who made the changes already had a paradigm of Jesus as their God. We will go to great lengths to make Jesus God because at this phase of our human evolution, we need a God with human traits like us.

One has to wonder how many changes such as these have occurred in the last two thousand years. I have seen in my lifetime well-meaning people make small, yet profound changes to the Bible that have altered significantly the very essence of what Jesus said.

All that a sincere seeker has to do is go to an Internet website on the Bible and compare verses side by side, like a parallel Bible, to see how slight changes in text can change the meaning of the verse. One of the most interesting examples of how just two words—*reign* and *heavens*—can change the meaning of a Bible verse is found in Matthew 11:11.

The King James Version of Matthew 11:11 states:

"Verily I say unto you, among them that are born of women there hath not risen a greater than John the Baptist: notwithstanding he that is least in the kingdom of heaven is greater than he."

Whereas Young's Literal Translation of Matthew 11:11 reads:

"Verily I say to you, there hath not risen, among those born of women, a greater than John the Baptist, but he who is least in the reign of the heavens is greater than he."

The phrase "least in the reign of the heavens" is much different from "least in the kingdom of heaven." Two synonyms for reign are supremacy and sovereignty. There is a profound and significant difference between being least in the reign of the heavens and being least in the kingdom of heaven in terms of a soul's awareness of reality.

The innocence of the soul becomes a portion of the ego personality of a human to learn lessons that advance the soul in love and intelligence. We are created as souls with innocence, but as humans we are, in our eyes, born into sin, because once we start the journey as a human, we have committed many errors (sins) previously as a human in past incarnations—unless, of course, we are new souls that have never before incarnated on planet Earth.

Taking on a human body is an immense decision by a mature soul. I do not need to elaborate on the trials and tribulations of being human. Living on planet Earth as a human is a dramatic and often traumatic experience for most of us. The harsh experiences we live through have the potential to teach us lessons for eternity through the process of revelations that give us instant realizations.

Why would a loving God allow such harsh experiences? The belief that we have sinned against God due to the free will of humankind gives God little merit and does not stand up to logic and reasoning. If God knows all, and perfection is Infinite Awareness, why even give a spirit, soul, or a human the opportunity to reject its Creator? Does God test us to see if we love our Creator? Does unconditional love test us, or is it fear that demands a test of loyalty?

A human ego with all of its fears may demand a test of loyalty, but never the infinite Spirit for all of creation. The sins-against-God belief demands an omnipotent God with human qualities. Our human egos are so deceptive that they are able to create a God in their own image with human character traits, and then they get much of the world to worship those traits. Let us not condemn the human ego but see it as a temporal, unaware personality to allow us to participate in the drama of the physical world.

It would be easy to despise the ego, but we must not; it is serving its purpose and allowing us to experience life as a human to overcome the obstacles of physical existence. Overcoming these obstacles and human desires develops the soul. Once we see clearly, we realize that all sin is due to some level of ignorance. If all this self-centered existence is due to some form of ignorance, then where did this ignorance originate?

<u>The Origin of Ignorance Revealed:</u>
No innocence, no error
No error, no ignorance
No ignorance, no variation
No variation, no relative world

No relative world, no phenomena
No phenomena, no creation of other
No creation of other, no unique identity
No unique identity means we only see oneness.

**For God to express itself, God must create souls
innocent of their reality:**
Along with innocence comes
an error of our reality.
Along with error of our reality,
we display our ignorance.
Along with this ignorance comes
a variation of phenomena.
Along with variation, phenomena create
a relative world.
Along with a relative world is
a perception of a unique identity.
Along with a unique identity
is the awareness of self and others.
Along with the awareness of self and others
is manifestation defined.
Along with manifestation
is the expression of God's love
and intelligence.

**We as souls are the manifestation and expression of
God's infinite Oneness.**

For Oneness to create the perception of otherness requires us to be unable to perceive our true identity due
to our innocence of our reality. The Hindu sages define
the journey from perfect intelligence to ignorance, from
ignorance to knowledge, and from knowledge to perfect
intelligence as a circle. The reality is that a soul progressing from innocence to ignorance requires a desire to seek

knowledge and intelligence. This inner soul's longing to seek knowledge and perfection comes from spirit.

What was revealed to me after years of seeking the origin of ignorance is that innocence precedes ignorance due to the necessity of the creation process from Oneness to many souls. The process of Oneness becoming many souls requires that souls be created innocent and unaware of their perfect reality, which is God.

We must learn how to discern the slight but profound difference between innocence and ignorance. Innocence is simply *that we were not created to know that which is available to be known* (involution), and ignorance is merely *that we have not yet acquired that which is available to be known* (evolution). Once we take our first step to acquire knowledge and divine intelligence—when we eat from the tree of knowledge—we have moved from innocence to ignorance. We are always innocent in God's eyes because God sees us as spirit; the eyes of the unaware see sin and condemn us.

The reality of God's perfectly imperfect creation:

When we see sin in others, we are projecting our sins,
but only out of ignorance.
When we condemn others, we condemn ourselves,
but only out of ignorance.
When we judge others, we judge ourselves,
but only out of ignorance.
When we harm others, we harm ourselves,
but only out of ignorance.
When we spite others, we spite ourselves,
but only out of ignorance.
When we make war on others, we make war on ourselves,
but only out of ignorance.

5. IS IGNORANCE THE CULPRIT?

When one understands the origin of ignorance, then ignorance is not the culprit, but rather the outcome of an innocent soul seeking perfection. Each soul is indwelled with a spirit (essence) that whispers thoughts of perfection to its consciousness. God, who is All in All, cannot create a consciousness of other without having an essence of itself within its creation's vital core (i.e., the spirit within that Jesus taught).

This essence of the Isness of God is spirit. This spirit moves an innocent soul to seek knowledge, and it is in this seeking that a soul's ignorance is revealed. Without our original innocence, there is no perception of self as a separate entity. Without seeking there is no ignorance revealed. It is this revealed ignorance that many call sin.

God experiences itself through the creation of innocent souls with unique identities. These unique identities, which we call souls, have levels of consciousness that feel and act separately from every other unique soul. It is important to understand that in order to experience, there must be a perception of other. Perfect awareness is not experiencing other. Perfect awareness is an understanding of self but not of other. A perception of other allows Oneness to express itself and its potential in an infinite variety of ways.

The Omnipresent creates infinite unique souls to experience its dynamic potential in a never-ending variety of experiences. God is omnipresent not only as an observer but as the spirit within us. The spark of awareness within us causes us to seek the divine love and intelligence of the Absolute. This is why it is fruitless to discuss whether God is within us or outside us. God is within us and outside us. How could Infinite Oneness *not* be?

The suffering that we experience here on earth is not of God; rather, it is our soul's longing to be perfect as the Father (God) in heaven is perfect. Because of that desire to be perfect, we experience life in a physical body with desires and survival instincts that are great challenges for the soul. We become actors on a world stage. This drama that we accept as reality gives our soul almost infinite opportunities to choose love over fear and to acquire divine intelligence. For most of us, only when we cross over to the astral world do we see this physical experience as a schoolroom.

Souls display their ignorance when they seek knowledge. The Old Testament authors must have known something about the origin of ignorance to write about Adam and Eve. I suspect a male wrote this story because the male ego blamed a woman for the desire to eat from the tree of the knowledge of good and evil. Taken literally, the Adam and Eve myth makes little sense, but taken as a parable or story, it may reveal our original innocence and the origin of ignorance to us. Little did I realize when I started my search for the origin of ignorance that the Adam and Eve story had some elements of truth?

We might state that the origin of our ignorance is the creation process. This would mean that God creates ignorant souls, and the absurdity of that statement is the ultimate heresy against God. Infinite Love and Intelligence does not create ignorant souls, but innocent souls. The underlying reality of the phenomenon we call ignorance is our eternal innocence.

Ignorance is a lack of knowledge, whereas innocence is *inexperience.* A new soul starts its journey as an expression of God with a lack of knowledge and experience. In religious terms, one could state that the eyes of God see our original and eternal innocence. The human mind much prefers being called a sinner than being told it is ignorant, because guilt is egocentric. Feeling guilty has its own reward to the human ego, which is a separate identity from God.

I have read that some spiritual teachers have called ignorance a tragic aspect of the human condition. God creates unique expressions of its love and intelligence, not tragic expressions. When a seeker sees this as a tragic aspect of the human condition, he or she is judging by appearances, and appearances can be very deceiving. The process of creating a unique soul as an expression of God is from innocence to ignorance to greater awareness of reality.

6. WHAT IS THE MEANING OF CREATION?

Infinite Oneness, being perfect awareness, would remain static and motionless without the process of creation. This process manifests itself in unique, living souls that change the infinite, yet static, Perfect Awareness (of God) into the dynamic realms of conscious beings. God expresses its dynamic potential through every living being. We as well as the evolving, unfolding universe are living proof of this dynamic aspect of God.

Why take the spiritual journey at all? Do we really have a choice with spirit whispering perfection to us? According to the mystics and the advanced spiritual teachings of spirits that have come through the mediumship of some truly great mediums, there is infinite peace waiting for each of us.

It is a journey of soul evolution. As we gain momentum in divine intelligence, we attain higher levels of consciousness. When a soul reaches higher levels of consciousness, compassion and creativity have expanded to a level that approaches our ultimate destiny.

We are gods in the making, contrary to what most religions teach. Our soul's ultimate destiny is to advance ever closer to the Infinite, which is That That Is. Often in this book, I have stated that we never lose our identity, which is the human ego's greatest fear. What we lose is our unawareness, which is the greatest of blessings.

For this book, we have defined God as the source of all love and intelligence. It makes sense to define God as perfect love and intelligence because it takes perfect intelligence to be fully aware of Self, and it takes perfect love to fully appreciate and value Self. The Source of all the underlying reality of the universe is perfect intelligence, and many call this Perfect Intelligence God. This Absolute is in a constant creative mode of being and becoming. God's very nature is to create and express itself through the manifestation of unique souls. If God did not create, God would be static, motionless, stationary, stagnant, and lifeless.

Some atheists ask that if it takes intelligence to create intelligence, who then created God's intelligence? Interesting question, but we must get into a place of no time, not the relative world, but the infinite, to realize that this question is invalid. Remember, infinite has no origin, whereas eternal does. God is infinite, and souls are eternal.

Some suggest that God does not even know its origin, so God creates as a way to discover itself continually. Scary thought to think that all of the pain and suffering of being human is for God to experience and/or discover itself. But the reality is that Oneness cannot express or share its love and intelligence unless it creates individual, conscious identities that perceive themselves as separate beings.

This Oneness, Cosmic Awareness, or Universal Consciousness expresses itself by manifesting infinite aspects of its very nature, which we call spirit. God creates innocent souls that progress toward awakening to their perfect love as they acquire perfect intelligence. Infinite has no origin, whereas eternal does, thus God is infinite. Souls are eternal because souls have a point of creation in reference to other souls. This means there are old souls/new souls and all levels of soul development in the universe.

God is and *God is That That Is* are two simple but compelling definitions of God. God as love and intelligence is more of a comprehensive operational definition of the qualities of God once we have valid definitions of love and intelligence. God as Infinite Love and Divine Intelligence is an acceptable operational definition for me. If you have a better definition of God, then go with it if it helps you have knowledge of the Oneness of God.

As some would say, there is nothing but God; all is God. Some believe that God is not the infinite God but a lesser god, and we are manifestations of that lesser god or gods. We are here to help this lesser god grow in love and divine intelligence. This could be a possibility, because continual, ongoing soul evolution (progress) in love and divine intelligence demands that we achieve godlike status. When we understand the evolution-of-the-soul process from a spark of awareness to greater levels of awareness, we see that indeed we might well be gods in the making as expressions of this Infinite Oneness.

It is not too much of a stretch of the imagination that a god or gods could manifest aspects of itself or themselves to achieve perfection. Meister Eckhart, the great Catholic mystic, preached about a Godhead, which did not act, and a God that created souls. This idea of lesser gods may explain his teachings. As souls evolve in consciousness, they also evolve in creativity; therefore, much of what we see as ongoing creation may indeed be the result of our souls having attained godlike status. (Note that godlike creative status is not God status.)

Whatever the case, whether God is expressing itself, sharing itself, experiencing itself, or discovering its potentiality, this does not take away from the reality of the love and intelligence of God. Most people consider the idea of a lesser god blasphemy, but they have not thought deeply that the continual progression of a soul demands that it progresses toward perfection. During that progression, we become as gods, not only knowing good from evil, but also having creative powers we can only imagine in our present level of consciousness.

A mature soul may decide to possess a human body with innate, egocentric desires to experience variation and phenomena on the physical level of existence. Many teach and have taught that souls are allowed to choose their fate to some degree by viewing aspects of their future life before they incarnate into a human body. The choices we make as humans help to determine our fate for future incarnations in the physical world. The level of love and divine intelligence in every choice we make determines our karma, which is one aspect of fate. Another aspect of fate might be the choices our soul makes between lives in the astral world. Fate creates experiences, experiences create karma, and karma guides a soul to choose love and compassion with every choice.

Choosing love in our decisions can be twofold: one is to awaken to our inner spirit and the other is to acquire perfect intelligence. Awakening and acquiring intelligence is an evolutionary journey for each unique soul. This evolutionary journey of the soul as a human is drama at its best: full of joy, suffering, misery, passions, creativity, insights, discoveries, learning, love, romance, error, anger, revenge, hate, judging, blaming, gratitude, and relationships—the list is almost endless.

What is difficult if not impossible to comprehend with our relative mortal minds is that Infinite Oneness does not lessen or reduce its wholeness by manifesting its essence (spirit) within each eternal soul during the creation process. Likewise, this Infinite Oneness (Godhead) does not gain or grow when a soul or lesser god draws ever closer to perfection, which of course is perfect love/intelligence.

The spirit within each soul guarantees our ultimate destiny. This spirit is perfection defined, and it will give us perfect directions, but we must listen. When Jesus said, "I can of mine own self do nothing: as I hear, I judge: and my judgment is just; because I seek not mine own will, but the will of the Father which hath sent me" (John 5:30 KJV Bible), he was talking about listening to his spirit. Absolute free will only exists at the spirit level, but then, of course, when we listen to spirit, it is God's will.

Necessity demands that each soul is created with original innocence and then, with time and experience, our ignorance is revealed to the world as errors and mistakes— and what many consider sin. Ignorance is considered a very negative word in our society. This is interesting because we are all ignorant of something to one degree or another. Most of our suffering is due to the soul's unawareness of its oneness with That That Is.

It helps us on our journey to keep in mind that ignorance is really the imperfections of our unawareness of perfect reality. There is no journey of the soul without unawareness; likewise, there is no creation of others without some degree of unawareness for each newborn soul.

Again, God is infinite. Infinite has no beginning or ending; it just is. Our mortal minds cannot fathom an existence without a beginning or end. God is sometimes referred to as Cosmic Consciousness, which is the underlying reality of all physical phenomena. I prefer the description of God as Cosmic Awareness or Infinite

Awareness, because awareness becomes consciousness during the creation process. Infinite is perfection defined. For Perfect Awareness to experience itself, it must manifest less than perfect aspects of its infinite Self. Eternal souls are created as expressions of infinite Spirit. God expresses itself through its creation, and we humans, as souls, are an aspect of that expression (i.e., creation and manifestation).

In the process of seeking, there are always false starts and frustrations. Every inventor knows this. It is the same when we seek intelligence. The challenge is not to be enticed into believing that one path to acquiring divine intelligence is more beneficial or faster than another path. There is always discord when we try to give unsolicited advice on which path should be taken.

Seek many paths or one path, but let life guide you. Listen to that inner voice and know that beliefs drown out that inner voice, so challenge everything that you carry in your bag of beliefs. Beliefs can weigh us down, and invalid beliefs slow our journey toward knowledge and intelligence.

The more intelligent we are—not intellectual, but intelligent—the more we are capable of loving ourselves. The more we love ourselves, the more we are capable of loving others. Older souls chose the path they are on to acquire intelligence. Newer souls may have just come crashing onto the scene from this incubator of souls we call nature. Why would a soul desire to attain intelligence? It takes intelligence to choose and demonstrate spiritual love, not intellectualism. The more we advance in spiritual love and compassion, the more we are capable of advancing in these higher dimensions after we cross over, as like attracts like.

7. IS FEAR THE OPPOSITE OR ABSENCE OF LOVE?

One of our greatest discoveries will be when educators realize the difference between intelligence and intellectualism. Then we will realize the causal correlation between love and intelligence. When we probe deeper, we will discover that fear is not the opposite of love, but the absence of love. It is so important to understand this because fear is a strong motivator, and since we judge by appearances, fear is often used as a motivator to enhance performance.

As a process and systems improvement consultant, I learned firsthand that pay for performance, which is taught in business schools, is fear based, and as such, it is a perfect example of how our unawareness can promote fear, competition, and hard feelings within an organization. Pay for performance is not based on systemic variation, but on an average line drawn in the center of the normal distribution of all employees' performances. This means that at all times, no matter how much the entire system has improved, at least half of the employees will be told to shape up or be threatened to ship out. This always creates a win/lose work or educational environment. Divine intelligence is not about creating winners and losers.

Fear changes our actions and thus appears to work as a motivator, but it creates resentment, negative side effects, and in the long term, is a destructive influence within an organization or educational institution. Fear as a motivator is based on influencing, whereas love is the basis of being influential. Likewise, intellectualism relies on influencing others, but being influential to others demonstrates intelligence. An example of someone demonstrating intelligence was Jesus, who was very intelligent and very influential in the world; his words still ring true today. When our actions are based in love, they are always an intelligent demonstration of compassion toward others and ourselves.

Fear may appear to be a good motivator, but it has ill side effects. The worst side effect is that it lowers our self-esteem. An interesting phenomenon is that low self-esteem does not lead to humility but rather causes us to go deeper into self-denial and be more critical toward others and ourselves. Self-criticism can lead to self-hate, and because our ego cannot endure this self-hate, it projects self-hate toward others in a variety of inappropriate ways.

When we look at history, we see that hate has created monumental suffering and misery for humankind. Our self-denial and self-hate can become so prevalent in our lives that we suffer deeply; it is in suffering that we often seek the meaning of life. Without our personal suffering, would we ever learn to have compassion for others and ourselves?

The more we fear, the more we move toward shyness or aggressiveness. A shy person is in fear and an aggressive person is in fear; they just chose different reactions to it. Metaphysical books break down our responses to the world as fear or love. The more we fear the lesser our capacity to love.

Religion misses the point when it says or suggests that we should fear God. A God of love would never need to be feared. Only an ego in its ignorance would fear God, never our soul looking through the eyes of the spirit within. Likewise, how could a God of infinite love and divine intelligence express wrath? I found many verses in the Old Testament and New Testament that state the word wrath in contexts such as "God's wrath" or "the wrath of God," (Examples: Nahum 1:2, Romans 1:18, John 3:36, KJV Bible). By all appearances, it may look like God is a wrathful and punishing God, but we have been warned by Jesus not to judge by appearances for a very good reason, as appearances can be misleading.

We often have made God in our image and given this Source of infinite intelligence human traits. We seem to need a human God, but for what reason? My observation is that having a God with human traits allows us to use our five senses and our ego's knowledge (intellect) of reality to attempt to perceive God.

Love is not emotional, but love can affect our emotions with a feeling of intense joy. The mystics tell us that love is a state of peace that surpasses understanding. Going beyond understanding boggles the mind. Our journey is a soul journey, and we can choose many lives to mature our souls to greater levels of love and divine intelligence.

Once we reach our destination of perfect love and intelligence, our state of being in the universe can only be speculated. My knowledge, based on an evolution-of-consciousness process, is that we move ever closer to Infinite Love and Intelligence. Some enlightened Hindus believe that we do not choose to join or merge with God; rather, we become That That Is. There is no choice, no sacrifice, no loss, and no decision—just being. Our personal journey is dynamic and in a constant state of working toward perfect love and intelligence.

Stating that we are gods in the making is not a popular thing to say to most people. It sounds egotistical and even arrogant, but I suspect that it is very egotistical to state that we are not gods in the making. I remember reading where a Sufi mystic stated something to the effect that saying we are children of God is very self-centered because we are claiming two existences: God and ourselves. The statement "I am God" may indeed be based on great humility, because we are stating that God is everything. Of course, we prefer the term that we are expressions of God; that still makes us a part of God and not separate entities, but living forms expressing God's infinite potential as souls.

Atheism and religion are systems of beliefs that depend much on dogma. And these beliefs are based in degrees of ignorance. Of course, we are kept in fear by an ego that thinks it knows reality. It is this fear that hinders our ability to love and to acquire intelligence. Fear closes our minds to accepting our own latent reality. Jesus referred to an Old Testament verse while responding to a question about his own godliness: "I have said, 'Gods ye [are], and sons of the Most High—all of you'" (Psalm 82:6 Young's Literal Translation).

The false self (the ego) is necessary for us to fully participate in the relative-phenomenal world, and I suspect even in these astral worlds in degrees of awareness for most of us. The ego keeps us involved in the drama of worldly affairs. There would be no experiencing the physical world without the ego, meaning some level of selfhood. This physical world gives us degrees of happiness/suffering, denial/acceptance, and pleasure/pain, but these experiences mold us as souls. Rather than condemn the ego, we must learn to appreciate its purpose and function. Its function is to give every soul diversified experiences that make every soul unique and that act and respond as individualized expressions of Infinite Oneness.

If we truly understand the significance of our ego, we have intelligence over it, and it does not dominate us, but serves us on our journey toward perfection. At the existing stage of our soul evolution, which surely is at the beginning stages, we need all the help we can get.

Many feel that they are old souls, but that is usually just their ego's influence over them. The good news is that the experiences we do have as humans are God's divine creation. We can't lose; we are sons of God and even become gods, as the Christian Bible correctly states in the New

International Version, Psalms 82:1, "God presides in the great assembly; he gives judgment among the 'gods.'" We all become the awareness and creative power of gods eventually; it depends on how often we choose love over fear and are of service to others. Choices based in love move us closer to God, whereas self-centered choices teach us lessons. Nothing is wasted. If an experience were not needed, it would not have occurred.

What we must take into consideration when we think about being an old soul or a new soul is that there are other planets with life far more advanced than ours; to not consider other planets with life on them in the universe is both arrogant and egotistical. We may be considered an old soul by earth standards, but a new soul by eternal soul standards.

This earth can only give us so many lessons, although the number of lessons is almost infinite, and they all aim to teach us love/intelligence. Mother Theresa is a supreme example of love/intelligence, rather than intellectualism. Her intellectual understanding of the world and other religions appeared not to be her greatest asset, but her love and her desire to serve others, which are attributes of love/intelligence, were enormous. As we progress in love/intelligence, we desire to learn advanced lessons and to serve others in need.

When a soul acquires status as an advanced soul, it may very well incarnate on this planet or another to point the finger to truth. Pointing others toward truth is an endeavor filled with trials and tribulations, and it very well may offer this advanced soul the opportunity to acquire even greater levels of divine intelligence. Furthermore, this advanced soul (mastermind) will have an opportunity to demonstrate compassion. Two enhanced attributes that increase our capacity to demonstrate compassion are awakening to our love within (spirit) and acquiring greater levels of divine intelligence.

God has attributes of supreme love and intelligence, so how do we know which came first, love or intelligence? The answer is neither, of course, because God is infinite. Well, that was no help, so let's try another approach. One could say that a baby has nothing but love and oneness in his or her heart; yes, a baby comes to us prepared to love the world, but a baby is more intelligent than we are. Simply put, a baby is intelligent, not intellectual. It takes years of social conditioning and innate but latent human desires to mask that love and replace it with intellectualism.

Richard Buckminster Fuller (1895–1983) stated that our schools were "ignorance factories." It is easy to be critical, but the beauty of the universe is that we are right where we need to be at this point of our human and soul evolution. As a favorite author of mine puts it, where would you go to school if your world known as planet Earth were perfect? Remember, our imperfections define us as unique souls, and two synonyms for unique are *distinctive* and *only one of its kind*. Our unique imperfections distinguish us from one another and from our Creator.

We must learn not to condemn ourselves, but to smile and love ourselves. (This is very difficult to do but easy to state.) If it were not a necessity for this Isness that most call God to express its potential, there would be no universe. Without realizing it, those who believe we have separated ourselves from God have little understanding of God's perfection. Their social and religious conditioning has distorted their thinking. We must learn to seek deeply into the spiritual reality of the relative-phenomenal world of appearances to fully appreciate our differences and our imperfections.

It sounds insane to state that we must learn to appreciate our imperfections, but without those imperfections, there is no us, just God. Of course, some souls have more imperfections than others have because there are all levels of soul development on this planet.

I attended a church with a friend one evening, and the preacher stated that God decides in advance who is going to heaven and who is going to hell for eternity. Who could possibly love a God with those traits? His sermon was more absurd than a sermon on free will. Free will only exists within the boundaries and limitations of ignorance. A saint once said that when we see the face of God, there is no longer any free will. What a remarkable understanding this saint had about human life and our connection to God to make that statement about the reality of free will. Intellectual knowledge and intellectualism seldom, if ever, reach that conclusion.

We do have the ability to respond, and this allows us to make choices. Those choices have boundaries, and those boundaries are our limited awareness, which can be overwhelmed by our misguided desires, and our lack of understanding that we are expressions of God and not separate from God. Believing that everyone, including ourselves, should always know right from wrong is a failure to understand that what some deem to be righteous choices and behavior often are harmful to themselves and others. The more closely our choices reflect love and divine intelligence, the more we see that it is not our will but God's that has the intelligence to guide us perfectly in our lives.

It may sound as if I am against intellectual knowledge, but the opposite is true; intellectual knowledge precedes intelligence, and not just in one lifetime, but many. Intellectual knowledge is one path to species development. Intelligence comes at what appears a very slow pace, but much intellectual knowledge can be gained in one lifetime for those who have the capability and interest.

My own doctorate degree is nothing more than an example of intellectual knowledge. It is easy for an ego to slip from intellectual knowledge to intellectualism, especially if that ego seeks recognition. That is why we often hear that college professors have little common sense. This is a simple example of confusing intellectual knowledge with intelligence. It is not common sense that most college professors lack, but divine intelligence. Before we judge them, we must first admit to our own lack of intelligence. Our greatest strength might be intellectual capacity, but sometimes this intellectual aptitude can become our greatest weakness if we allow our intellectual knowledge to become intellectualism.

Divine intelligence is based in truths, and truth is never a weakness because it is eternal. Truth will stand the test of time and intelligence. Stating truths may cause us to be harmed by others, but remember, we humans are temporal beings. Our souls seek these truths and are willing to live the harshness of human life to obtain them. Stated another way, a soul is willing to experience darkness to obtain light.

Without intellectual knowledge, the Western world and its technology would not exist. These technological advances are drawing the world together in so many ways. Someday I suspect we will be given the benefit of the intellectual knowledge and intelligence of life on other planets, and that will be like a jump-start toward having greater knowledge of our universe and ourselves. The day may come when we can communicate using electronic devices with those on the other side. Edison tried it and failed, but George Meek, a sincere seeker into the paranormal who spent hundreds of thousands of dollars to test it, tried it and succeeded to some degree.

Two truths exist in the universe: love and divine intelligence. If we want to have knowledge of our purpose, our being, and our universe, then we need to strive to see the value in discovering the subtle but profound difference between self-confirming, egotistical love, and selfless, spiritual love, as well as the difference between intellectual knowledge and divine intelligence.

Learning these differences will change the way we educate our children, manage our organizations, preach our sermons, and accept our diversity. Example: diversity is our greatest friend on our soul's evolutionary journey, and yet at this phase of our human evolution, most treat it as something to avoid. Racism is living with ignorance. Not only is it an example of our lack of intelligence; it also an example of our lack of love for self and others.

People and societies who kill one another over land, resources, and religious beliefs do not realize that they are killing their brother and sister souls. As souls, we are all unique creations of God. Our eternal self is our soul. As souls, we are all related to the one Source of all creation, which is God. We are all souls created by God. God does not have favorites, but we humans in our ignorance do. Those who think God has the ability to have chosen people or religions have succumbed to self-centered beliefs that they are separate selves from God. The ego will create some pretty interesting drama to validate itself as separate and special.

Diversity enhances creativity, and creativity is based in intelligence. When I teach seminars, I find that more creativity surfaces when the group is more diverse. This creativity is released through dialogue and facilitation. Think of it this way: in our ignorance, we have had severe problems with diversity, but it is through problems that we have learned valuable lessons—slowly, I know, but we have progressed on our soul journey and human development. Problems are the perfect feedback, not only on a personal level but also on a mass level, to enhance our knowledge as humans, countries, societies, nations, and as souls toward love/intelligence.

Problems are lessons that give us opportunities to learn and gain insights. These insights improve our probability to receive a realization and to advance in love and intelligence. Have you ever noticed in life that as soon as we work through one problem, another one surfaces? Recurring problems can soon wear us down. Those seeking enlightenment that sit on a mountaintop or in a cave and refuse to participate in the world may have missed the value of human life. They may reincarnate on this planet or another to learn greater levels of divine intelligence as expressions of God that we call human life.

8. WHAT KEEPS US FROM ASKING THESE PROFOUND QUESTIONS?

I am amazed at our ego's deceptive abilities, because when wars are fought, both sides think God is on their side. After the terrorist attack on September 11, 2001, many people in America said "God bless America" and put bumper stickers with this slogan on their cars without realizing that God does not have chosen people or nations. As hard as it is to understand, Infinite Love and Intelligence bless us all, as we are all innocent in the eyes of God. The terrorists who conducted the attack shouted before they died, "God is great!" They thought, of course, that they had earned favors with God for killing those who did not adhere to their religious beliefs. Their beliefs were egocentric and an ignorant view of the reality of Oneness.

I wonder how many who put God bless America stickers on their bumpers and who read this previous paragraph will see the terrorists' ignorance but will be unable to see their own self-centered beliefs found in stating, "God bless America." I do not wish to imply by these statements that a self-centered belief of putting God bless America on our vehicles is as destructive as becoming a terrorist, but both are based on different levels of self-centeredness and an unawareness of the oneness of our divine reality.

Because our egos believe they are special, and nations consist of a collection of egos, nations can come to believe that they are special, even to the point of believing that they have been *chosen*. The beliefs of any nation that proclaims it is God's chosen people or nation are the result of collective egos in action and not the reality of perfect love and divine intelligence.

I do not want to appear unpatriotic here. The point I am making is that the blessings of God are on all nations as we are all expressions of this Infinite Oneness. Patriotism and nationalism can become ego centered and blind us to all others' divine reality.

The mode of being in this world that prevents us from asking the *right* questions is as follows: we have been created without knowledge of our original innocence, which is ignorance. The greatest inhibitor to acquiring knowledge is our believing that we have asked the right questions and that we already possess the right answers. There are multitudes of reasons why we ask invalid questions, including arrogance, pride, conditioned beliefs, intellectualism, fear of embarrassment, and, of course, we simply have yet to learn what questions to ask.

9. WHAT IS THE DIFFERENCE BETWEEN EGO, SOUL, SPIRIT, AND GOD?

Ego: The ego is an aspect of our human personality based on our social conditioning since birth. Family, society, religion, education, and every significant moment in our physical lives create our individual egos. The ego is unable to justify its existence until it begins to realize its purpose and its connection to its ultimate reality, which is the ability to respond and to live life as a unique expression of God.

The ego lives in fear of losing itself either to the awakening of our soul or death. It will do almost anything to promote itself as a separate reality. The ego appears to have unlimited talent in self-deception, vanity, and denial. Very few in the world come to understand the power their ego has over their thoughts and actions. There are common characteristics between the soul and the ego, so separating observed phenomena as either soul centered or ego centered is difficult to determine now in our evolutionary journey.

Most choices are ego centered. From the ego's point of view, everyone and everything is here for it. As an individual and as a society become more advanced in unconditional love and divine intelligence, the choices the ego makes will be in more alignment with our souls' consciousness and spiritual awareness. The dividing line between how influential our soul and ego are in the choices we make will lessen. The universe is dynamic, and our ego can progress just as the soul can. Of course, a society can become more egocentric, even to the point of self-destruction. There is no guarantee of the survival of any species, including ours.

There can be no extinction of the soul because the soul is eternal.

The ego can be our best friend, but it can also be our worst enemy. It is our best friend because it gives the soul the drama of human experiences. The ego aids us in our journey by helping us to discern the difference between truths and false or invalid teachings. The human experience is often harsh, but this harshness allows choices, always with consequences, that can be beneficial to the soul.

Overcoming adversity develops the soul. The ego can appear to be our worst enemy if we fail to recognize its purpose. Treating the ego as the enemy can create a go-to-war intellectual approach to life. Some synonyms for war are as follows: conflict, combat, warfare, fighting, confrontation, hostilities, and battle. These attributes do not bring us peace but force us deeper into a denial of our own reality. When I hear the term spiritual warriors from some pastors, I realize that the term is a prime example of an oxymoron.

The teaching to turn the other cheek has been lost on these preachers. They want to do God's work for God, as God is not working fast enough for them. The greatest change we can make in the world is to change ourselves from within. The ego is not our enemy, and it can be our greatest asset if we lose interest in our selfish and fearful ways and experience ourselves as expressions of God. The survival instinct of being human can make the ego very fearful and selfish. The soul must pass through this phase on its evolutionary journey.

Those who advocate obliterating the ego or removing the ego have failed to see the ego's role in soul evolution. Our choice is how long we want to allow the ego to rule our lives. We must smile at our self-centeredness and not go to war with our self-centered viewpoint of the world.

Our ego allows us to have self-centered experiences, and those experiences all have decision points that give us opportunities to choose love over fear and to acquire divine intelligence over ignorance. Of course, an intelligent choice is always a choice for love; likewise, a choice for love is always an intelligent choice.

If we make the ego our foe, we get caught up in the battle. It is far better to seek knowledge and understanding of the ego and realize it is a temporal and a fearful shadow of reality that shares ownership of the physical body with our soul. Its whole design and function is to be self-centered to survive, because it is part of nature with a survival instinct.

Soul: The soul is our essence and is astral in that it exists as an energy field. Many call this energy field our aura. Or aura changes colors as our soul evolves and progresses in love and divine intelligence. We had a soul before we were born into the physical world as a human, and our soul is with us throughout our eternal life as an entity. The soul is eternal because it was created by the Infinite Source of all that is.

Each soul is unique, therefore original. It is revealing to look at some synonyms for the word original: unique, authentic, creative, novel, unusual, and imaginative. No other soul has ever existed or will ever exist that is exactly like our soul. This statement in itself should give anyone a deeper faith and love for the profound intelligence of this Isness we call God.

The creation of an original soul demands that soul's original innocence.

Innocence is inexperience, and this inexperience reveals itself as ignorance, which reveals itself as the phenomena of sin and evil. In the eyes of Perfect Awareness that soul's original innocence is also its eternal innocence.

Perfect awareness has righteous judgment, but with our soul's limited awareness, we see the phenomena of sin and evil and not the underlying reality of them, so we lack righteous judgment. By *righteous judgment* we mean blameless judgment. "Judge not according to the appearance, but by *righteous judgment*" (John 7:24, KJV Bible).

What is appearance but phenomena? To come to know not only our original innocence but also our eternal innocence, we must see righteous judgment as blameless judgment. The human mind will find blameless judgment extremely difficult, as the world teaches us otherwise on a daily basis. Difficult is not impossible, however, and there is assurance that the day will come when we will see our eternal innocence. Only in our unawareness of reality do we ignore that which is available to be known.

Why is it that humankind has ignored a key synonym for righteousness, which is blamelessness? Is it because we have made God in our image, and we see God as a deity that judges its creation? What does exist is our own susceptibility to self-judgment.

When we cross over, we receive a life review, and we will not only review our selfish acts in our lives, but also the pain we have caused others from our actions. The divine principle that what we sow, we reap can feel like judgment because of the possible suffering it creates in our lives. With this suffering, we can learn to express compassion, which is blameless judgment. Blameless judgment is based in understanding the underlying reality of others' actions and our own.

Think of nature as an incubator for souls. Consciousness evolves from a spark of awareness, so there will be a phase of judgment toward self and others that every soul must pass through on its journey of expanding love and divine intelligence. The cycle of soul creation and development is the involution of spirit and evolution of the soul. The soul has a tremendous advantage over the ego because most human souls have had many lives to learn love/intelligence. The soul was created in a state of innocence of its divine reality. It had loving guides to care for it from the moment of its creation, and it had perception of self and other.

A soul must be created innocent of its divine reality, as understanding cannot be given, but must be earned. Even knowledge comes to us through the process of the variation of contrasting conditions in our lives. We learn light (divine intelligence) from the interactions of light and darkness, which some might call good and evil. This process of serial experiences with choices that give us the element of time coupled with consequences for those choices not only develops the soul, but it makes every soul unique.

Those who say time is an illusion fail to see the necessity of this process of serial experiences that matures the soul to greater levels of divine intelligence. Some religious Eastern spiritual teachers have stated that our lives are just an illusion. They fail to see that we as souls are not illusions but are expressions of God. As expressions of God, we are not illusions but dynamic expressions of the infinite attributes of Infinite Oneness. To call us illusions is to say that God creates illusions. How interesting it is that some believe that they are only illusions.

If one thinks deeply on how someone could believe he or she is only an illusion, one will find this statement is based in religious intellectualism. As souls, we are not illusions, but our experiences (phenomena) are temporal and transient. Two synonyms for illusion are *fantasy* and *trick*, and as souls, we are not a fantasy or a trick of God. We are divine expressions of God. As an experiment, look into the eyes of a young child or a newborn baby and tell yourself that he or she is just an illusion. He or she is a miracle from God, and to call him or her an illusion is the very definition of intellectualism, which of course has its origin in ignorance.

The soul in the astral world does not have to deal with human desires and fears. The soul has not become perfect, as some claim. If it were, there would be no need for that soul to incarnate in physical form to acquire divine intelligence.

There are souls at all levels of the evolution-of-consciousness process. I believe that most of us here on planet earth with a few exceptions are beginning to medium souls. During my research, many people told me that they thought they were old souls, but I think this belief is often a worldly status-quo idea that is egocentric.

I found very few people in my years of research that understood how much their egos influenced their behaviors, beliefs, paradigms, and actions in this world. I have met several people who claim that their goal in life is to make their children and others happy, which they believe makes them a positive and helpful presence in the world. Many of these people took various prescription drugs in order to cope, and they lived very unhappy lives. The deception of our egos can be very harmful to our modes of being in this world.

The soul cannot be defined as an infinite entity, but it can be defined as eternal. The spirit that dwells within each soul is infinite because it comes from the Infinite and is an aspect or fragment of God. Souls advance toward perfection. The number of incarnations of each soul into this physical world is impossible to know at this stage of our understanding and soul evolution.

Spirit: Spirit is an aspect or fragment of God within us. The spirit sustains us with God's vital energy and perfect awareness. This spirit within us is the lifeblood of our existence. Without spirit, we would cease to exist as consciousness and awareness. Spirit is infinite whereas soul is eternal. Every soul has a divine and holy spirit that guarantees eternity. God's blueprint to evolve souls in love and divine intelligence is flawless.

The spirit within every soul creates for that soul a longing to draw ever closer to its creator. Because of the indwelling spirit within each soul, God shares with our soul perfect awareness. Because the soul has less than perfect intelligence, it fails to recognize this perfect awareness within the very core of its being. Whereas the soul is in process of becoming ever closer to perfection, the spirit is infinite; therefore, it is perfection. God placed an aspect of its perfection inside a very hidden and veiled place: within us.

God: God is. God is All in All. God is Oneness. God is the infinite source that provides the vital force (energy) for all that is. The infinite source of all that is can best be described but not perfectly defined as Infinite Love and Divine Intelligence. God is perfect awareness. Perfect awareness sees clearly, and this awareness has a dynamic potential that creates a consciousness of other (involution) to express its qualities of love and intelligence. Perfect Awareness has no beliefs, no filters, no attachments, no agenda, no plan, and no ignorance; God is simply perfect awareness.

A person cannot comprehend God, define God, or even imagine God, but one can become aware of the qualities of God. To be aware of God's qualities of love and divine intelligence is to love thy neighbor as thyself, which is not emotional love, but selfless love. The closest word our dictionaries have for selfless love is agape love. Love without expectations is selfless love.

I work with four-year-old children, and when I am swinging them and they look at me with those precious smiles on their faces, it is like looking into the face of God. I see innocence, true joy, and love within their smiles and laughter. Every child is a miracle, and for some to state that this miracle child is here due to a chance occurrence of lighting hitting a puddle of slime is truly ignorance defined. Likewise, stating that a child has fallen from the grace of God and a sacrifice is needed to redeem that child is also ignorance defined. But we must always keep within our hearts and minds that ignorance has its origin in our original innocence.

The five senses cannot comprehend God, but consciousness can be aware of God. Atheists are atheists because they rely on their five senses and intellectual abilities to perceive reality. The five senses are unable to perceive the underlying reality of the relative-phenomenal world. Likewise, intellectual ability can often become intellectualism, and thinking we know when we do not hinders our ability to perceive a supreme intelligence. This intellectualism prevents us from seeing miracles occurring around us every day of our lives.

As Thoreau said, "it is not what you look at that matters, it is what you see."

As long as we believe that love is an emotion or a feeling, we will continue to give God human traits. As Mark Twain said, "God created man in his image and man returned the favor." It may take several years into a search for truth before the seeker realizes that humanity has made God in its image. We desire a God with human traits and appearance because it allows us to perceive God with our five senses and our intellect.

Many Eastern sages teach that if a soul can acquire this perfect awareness, then the soul becomes That That Is. Even in this scenario, there is no annihilation of the individual identity of a soul because the soul's identity becomes perfect awareness. This is a very important point to consider, because the fear of annihilation of our personality can cause us to miss some very important opportunities to awaken to some insights and discoveries in our spiritual quest for truths. Fear of anything can cloud our thinking, and this fear of losing our identity or uniqueness to nothingness hinders our ability to see outside our circle of beliefs.

For this book, the two attributes of God have been defined as perfect love and divine intelligence. Intelligence is not an IQ test. An IQ test measures what we know and how fast we learn. In this book, we refer to those attributes as the intellect. Intellectual capacity and capability have much to do with human evolution and genetics because intellectual capacity is a function of the brain. Genetics plays a very important role in the attributes of the intellect, as well they should.

A person can be very smart and have a high IQ but not be very intelligent. Think of intelligence as divine understanding. Intelligence is a measure of our compassion and our ability to perceive spiritual truths. If we are to define God's attributes as love and intelligence, then we must redefine the word intelligence. This is no easy task for the reader because we have been conditioned to believe that smart people are intelligent. Intellectual capability (aptitude) is based on knowledge and the time it takes to learn that knowledge, whereas intelligence is the ability to perceive the hidden and divine meanings of life.

Valid concepts transform our consciousness. They set the stage for realization to occur through the process of a revelation. Valid concepts can heal us physically and mentally because they are based in truth. Truth is self-validating. Invalid concepts cause immeasurable suffering in this world because they are based in ignorance. Remember, ignorance is an unawareness of our true reality.

10. HOW DID YOU APPROACH YOUR QUEST FOR ANSWERS TO THE MYSTERY OF LIFE?

I knew that I enjoyed reading and doing research, so I read and reread many different sources in the areas of theoretical quantum physics, Christianity, Hinduism, Sufism, Buddhism, Kabbalah, mysticism, spiritualism, new thought, and the enlightened ones. Also, I studied philosophy, leadership, quality improvement, atheist materials, books about channeling, psychics/mediums, books written by mediums, and so on. I also read several books on reincarnation, karma, past and between-life regression using hypnosis, out-of-body experiences, and near-death experiences.

I discovered a spiritual jewel, a little known book in a used bookstore about a medium that had exceptional mediumship abilities. He kept his mediumship private and only sought spiritual knowledge. This medium was able to receive, while in a deep trance state, spiritual teachings from an intelligence that existed in a highly developed spiritual dimension.

After the medium passed, his wife, who had kept those teachings in a blanket chest, wrote a book about her life with her husband, and she included those teachings in her book. In my quest for spiritual truths, these teachings have been the most advanced I have found about the many mysteries of life. I have been studying these teachings almost daily for more than twelve years.

I have read many books several times and have found new insights with each reading. I have attended several study groups such as A Course in Miracles and Conversations with God, and I have lived short periods with Hindu and Buddhist monks. I stayed for a short time in a Catholic monastery that had an extensive library with many books written by and about Catholic, Hindu, Buddhist, and Sufi mystics.

I also spent time utilizing my small off-road vehicle to go deep into the Arizona Mountains and desert to find a beautiful place for introspection and meditation, and to pray for guidance. These trips were a blessing because of the beauty of the mountains and the high desert; they gave me a respite from the drama of organizational consulting and a sense of peace that I was unable to find in the fast pace of city life.

I asked many questions about people's beliefs during conversations with them at formal and informal gatherings. I spent a lot of time on the Internet chatting with people about their views on life, and life after death. Because I was a consultant, I traveled all over the United States and spent some time in Japan and Europe, and this travel allowed me to achieve a good cross-section of people and their beliefs.

This may sound insane, but with any intellectual and spiritual search for truth, it is beneficial to study theoretical quantum physics. The following is what I discovered in my search. Physicists who seek deeper into the science of physics often decide to study quantum physics. Quantum physicists who seek the deeper mysteries of the micro universe often study theoretical quantum physics.

Theoretical quantum physicists often sound like philosophers in their statements about the reality that they construct from their experiments and research. When they seek a deeper understanding of life than philosophy can provide, they become spiritual seekers, and their statements about the quantum universe sound more mystical than scientific.

Quantum physics defies explanation until we factor in an underlying reality beyond the physical. It is discoveries like the quantum that may bring science and religion together in the future. It is interesting to see how a seeker in science can become a spiritual seeker if he or she is able to move beyond his or her materialistic beliefs.

I call these materialistic beliefs one's circle of beliefs, and it is almost impossible for us to think outside of our own circle of beliefs. Draw a circle and put all of your known beliefs inside of it, and you will have your circle of beliefs. Some call this a box of beliefs and say to think outside the box if you want to create new ideas. From my reference the universe has more to do with circles than boxes, but either concept makes the point of how restricted we are by our beliefs.

I have an acquaintance who gives presentations on thinking outside the box. Would anyone like to guess how well this person does thinking outside of his own box of beliefs? Any consultant worth his or her consulting fees knows that often we need to learn what we teach. My experience with consultants and professors suggests that education is no guarantee of having an open mind, but there are exceptions.

I learned that any serious seeking of the metaphysical aspects of the universe reveals that there is more to this world than meets the eye. Saint Paul said, "So we fix our eyes not on what is seen, but on what is unseen. For what is seen is temporary, but what is unseen is eternal" (2 Corinthians 4-18, NIV Bible). "Seek and you shall find" is valid guidance. Seeking with a minimum of preconceived notions and with an unbiased viewpoint will reveal much more to the seeker. Always remember that at this stage of our human and soul development, we are not immune to a biased viewpoint.

As humans, we experience this relative-phenomenal world in an infinite variety of ways. As stated earlier, this relative world gives us variation, whereas the phenomenal world gives us temporal experiences (phenomena). Think of this world as a soul enhancer. Without it, where would a soul go to school? One of my great personal discoveries has been that through reincarnation, as Plato stated, with each new life we pass through the river of forgetfulness, so we are able to experience this world anew as humans.

Ego eyes condemn the world as sinful, but mature soul eyes smile at the world and view it as a journey to soul perfection. If you think perfection is beyond your reach and you are a Christian, remember that Jesus taught that perfection is possible.

We never lose our longing for the infinite and for attaining greater awareness. This desire toward the infinite is spirit whispering to our souls and egos to come home. The illusion of separation to the ego often manifests itself as an inner loneliness, so we often "sin" to overcome this feeling of separation. This sin could be described as looking for love and acceptance in all the wrong places. But remember it is often these wrong places that give us experiences that have the opportunity to teach us lessons about our divine reality.

There are no mistakes; if an experience were not needed, it would not have occurred. All experiences take us closer to Divine Love and Intelligence. The world teaches us both good and bad, but in the realm of reality, all experiences, even misguided experiences, have the opportunity to educate the soul to greater awareness. How can this be? What we view as a failure is often the greatest of learning experiences. When we look back on our lives, we see these "failures" had much to teach us.

11. HOW DOES PERFECT AWARENESS DIFFER FROM CONSCIOUSNESS?

To answer this question, we need to examine ignorance. It is such a negative word in our society, but the reality is that ignorance is simply a synonym for unawareness. Human unawareness has its home in our original innocence. Innocence is a conscious being that lacks perfect intelligence, whereas ignorance is the demonstration of a lack of perfect intelligence. Ignorance is having not yet acquired perfect, divine intelligence.

The reality of ignorance is that anyone who does not have perfect intelligence has some ignorance within his or her consciousness. Anyone who has been created with imperfect divine intelligence will commit errors, and most of the world will call those errors sin. Then, of course, if we believe that errors are a sin against God, we will label those who commit such errors as evil or sinful people.

As a soul's awareness expands, it makes better choices, and therefore it commits fewer errors. A soul that has attained perfect divine intelligence is without error. This soul has moved beyond what we know as consciousness to perfect awareness. It may be helpful to think of consciousness as a manifestation of perfect awareness.

12. ARE YOU SAYING THAT CONSCIOUSNESS AND AWARENESS ARE DIFFERENT?

Yes, that is exactly what I am saying. They are different in the sense that awareness is the ultimate reality, whereas consciousness is our created reality. The Infinite Source of all intelligence creates unique souls. These unique souls have consciousness, which gives the perception of other. Awareness is who we are as spiritual beings; it is our divine reality, whereas consciousness is our created reality.

This is why many Eastern sages call life on earth an illusion, because it is not our primary reality. The illusion is a perception of other, and this requires a certain level or degree of unawareness. There is only one reality: Infinite is All in All. The very definition of Infinite is that it has no boundaries.

Physical life is not an illusion; it is a necessary dimension or step for the journey of the soul, and that journey is a unique expression of God. We as expressions of God are divine, and we cannot be separate from the infinite Source of all that is or ever will be. A journey demands a starting point, and the journey of the soul's origin is its innocence of its divine reality.

Think of consciousness as awareness with cataracts and wearing blinders, because consciousness does not see with clarity; it perceives only a small, cloudy part of reality. Anyone who has had cataract surgery knows what it is like when the bandage is removed from the eye after surgery. A new, bright, and colorful world exists, which gives one a new awareness of reality. As truths are revealed to our soul's consciousness, we see reality much more clearly and with a wider focus, and we see a much more beautiful and loving world.

The journey toward infinite and perfect awareness is an awakening process that removes our blinders and clears our vision so that we may see better and discern the underlying reality of all appearances. It is the realization of universal truths that awaken us to the infinite love within our consciousness. We acquire divine intelligence and perfect love by the realization of these universal truths.

The acquiring of truths is divine intelligence defined. The intelligence I am speaking about is the infinite intelligence of God, not intellectual ability or aptitude. Intellectual knowledge can be achieved by effort and learning. Likewise, we can inherit intellectual capability from our parents. Divine intelligence comes to us through the process of a revelation that gives us a realization. When our minds are open to receive, a truth will be revealed to us.

Human consciousness is one level below soul consciousness, but of course, all consciousness has a degree of awareness within it because awareness is the essence of spirit. Human consciousness has less awareness of its spiritual essence than soul consciousness has. The process of acquiring intelligence advances our souls to higher levels of consciousness, and we become increasingly more awakened to our indwelling spirits. Our soul consciousness continues to progress toward perfect intelligence. This evolutionary journey toward perfection is best described as soul evolution.

Consciousness and awareness are the stuff of life, but consciousness has a perception of other, whereas awareness has an understanding of self as Oneness. If God created us with perfect awareness, we would not have a separate identity or see others as different from us.

The only person who can answer the question correctly about awareness and consciousness is someone who understands the origin of our unawareness, which is our original blamelessness. We as souls cannot take personal responsibility for our creation, as we are but expressions of the Creator. Without this understanding of the origin of ignorance, we will see awareness as an aspect of consciousness. One of my premises during my years of research and study was that perfection would only create imperfection if it desired to do so.

Ask yourself the following question: How could perfection create anything imperfect unless it desired to do so? The imperfections that make us unique began as our created limited awareness. Every soul's journey is from imperfection to perfection. That journey is the expression of God.

Consciousness has a personal identity and is but an aspect of perfect awareness, whereas perfect awareness sees only Oneness. This Oneness or "Being" is what most of us call God. God shares and experiences itself by the creation of souls with less than perfect intelligence. Because God creates souls with these characteristics, there is a certainty that all souls and humans are innocent of their reality and unable to make perfect choices.

We were created in innocence, and we remain innocent during our entire evolutionary journey toward infinite perfection. It is important to remind oneself that souls are always innocent during this journey to greater awareness and on the journey back to Oneness. A most profound question to ask is this: If a soul can indeed return to its Source of creation, which is God, can an aspect or an expression of Infinite return to God? Maybe infinite is unobtainable; maybe it isn't. Each reader will have to decide for him or herself the answer to that profound question.

Always know that we never lose our identity; our identity may change but it is never sacrificed. We are never nothingness because nonexistence is impossible. Most spiritual teachings reveal that a soul can always retain its personal identity when it desires to do so, even when it has chosen to reside in a group soul environment. It is extremely difficult to find souls in these higher realms of existence to reveal their wisdom to a physical medium with a lower level of consciousness development. History has given us rare instances when spirits from these higher dimensions (Jesus's mansions) come through a medium and reveal to the world the very essence of spiritual wisdom.

The worst sinner who has committed the most severe evil acts known to humanity is innocent in God's eyes. Perfect Love and Intelligence loves us and accepts us unconditionally. Anyone who tells you otherwise has succumbed to his or her ego and has failed to understand the origin of ignorance and the perfection of God. Our eternal innocence exists because Infinite cannot duplicate its infinite awareness.

Please do not confuse innocence with a lack of suffering. Our choices can and do bring suffering into our lives. The ego despises the reality that all souls are innocent because the ego judges by appearances. Culpability, with its first cousin, guilt, is the mainstay of the human ego. The term personal responsibility is code for culpability and blameworthiness. Even the atheist who refuses to believe in a Supreme Source of love and intelligence has an ego that wants to be special by maintaining that he or she has no creator. The atheist considers his or her ego personality the ultimate reality. It is very egoistical and self-righteous to believe that the human ego is our ultimate reality.

13. WHAT IS OUR ULTIMATE REALITY?

Ultimate reality is Spirit, which is Perfect and Pure Awareness. Spirit is synonymous with God, whereas consciousness is synonymous with the soul. Consciousness is a flow of thoughts intertwined with moments and degrees of self-awareness. During meditation, ask yourself who or what is observing your flow of thoughts. In time, you will discover that this awareness of self is the observer of your thoughts. Is reality the observer or the flow of thoughts?

We are innocent of our reality because we lack the ability to experience the complete essence of perfect awareness within our spirit. God experiences itself by manifesting its Spirit within us and by creating a consciousness with a perception of other. The creation process is a great mystery until we understand the relationship between awareness and consciousness.

As we attain knowledge about the origin of ignorance, we see this connection between awareness and consciousness. It is important to contemplate and reflect on the difference between these two expressions of life to understand the mysteries of life.

Consciousness has a certain level or degree of awareness, but not perfect awareness. God has perfect awareness; souls have degrees of awareness, dependent on its evolutionary progress. Most humans lack awareness of the divine spirit within them, and have minimal awareness of their soul.

The soul that resides within us often has a higher level of intelligence within its consciousness than our human ego. Human life with its creeds, beliefs, and dogmas can overpower the intellect of the human mind. These aspects of life in the physical world most often create a human personality that can overpower the intelligence of our soul. This overpowering of the soul by our ego personality is ignorance in action and creates much suffering in our lives. The root cause or origin of our suffering is ignorance.

Most of the world condemns this ignorance in action because they fail to see the very reason a soul incarnates into a human body. A soul comes to Earth to acquire divine intelligence by participating in the drama of human life. The drama of being human provides opportunities for advancement in unconditional love and divine intelligence.

This drama of living the life of a human in a physical body with all of its limitations has much suffering and joy, and both suffering and joy, like successes and failures, offer each soul an opportunity for growth in unconditional love and divine intelligence. Our suffering can often teach us levels of sympathy that can, over time and serial experiences, advance to empathy and then to levels of compassion. Compassion is rare, as compassion is based on understanding, not feelings. I have heard it stated many times that we learn light from darkness, and there is often much truth in that statement.

14. WHY WOULD GOD CREATE A PERSON WITH A CONSCIOUSNESS THAT LACKS PERFECT AWARENESS?

I have discovered that the only people who can answer this question correctly are the ones who have knowledge or understanding about the origin of ignorance. Without this knowledge or understanding of the origin of ignorance, we believe that we have fallen from the grace of God, disobeyed God, or fallen asleep to our ultimate reality. With this mindset, we will continually see ourselves as separate from God and not expressions of this infinite Isness.

Ask yourself the following question: How can the perfection of God create anything imperfect unless it desires or has a necessity to do so? As a meditation exercise, spend time contemplating the following question: if God created us with perfect awareness, what would be our identity? The answer to that question will help to reveal that the origin of our ignorance is our original innocence.

Consciousness has a personal identity and is but an aspect of perfect awareness, whereas perfect awareness sees only Oneness. This Oneness, or what many refer to as Cosmic Consciousness, is what most of the world calls God. God shares and expresses itself through our experiences by the creation of souls with less than perfect intelligence—a necessary process to ensure that all souls are created with original innocence and therefore are unable to make perfect choices.

Our original innocence is our unawareness. We are not our own creators. Our very uniqueness as souls exists due to a process of the involution of awareness and the evolution-of-consciousness process.

As souls, we were created innocent of our perfect reality; therefore, we are always innocent in the "eyes" of Perfect Awareness (God). This is our eternal innocence. The world will protest violently that we cannot be eternally innocent as they see sin and evil in the world as human culpability, but the world confuses phenomena with our true and perfect reality, which is spirit. It is important to note here that phenomena are not an illusion, for that which manifests from the Real is itself real but temporal and transient.

Most of the world spends little if any time on the nature of reality. We judge by appearances, which are phenomena. If we consider sin and evil as phenomena and nothing more, we realize that they have their home in our unawareness of reality. This unawareness can also be called ignorance. Plato was correct when he wrote, "Ignorance [is] the root and stem of every evil." This unawareness begins in the creation process, as does our original innocence. Our original unawareness is a mandatory condition for souls to evolve and progress as unique (only one of a kind) expressions of this infinite Isness most call God.

15. HOW CAN YOU STATE THAT SOULS ARE ALWAYS INNOCENT?

We were created in innocence, and we remain innocent during our entire evolutionary journeys toward infinite love and divine intelligence. It is important to remind oneself that souls are always innocent during this journey toward greater and expanding levels of awareness of their spiritual reality.

Our eternal innocence does not imply that social justice is not needed in this world of phenomena. Without social justice, the physical imperfect world would be in chaos as we humans still have a very low level of awareness as to our reality as spiritual beings.

We are learning, we are attaining knowledge, and we are gaining wisdom. With this wisdom, we must apply the universal principle that we reap what we sow. We can reap the consequences of suffering or joy depending on the choices we make, whether they are based on love or misguided desires. It is as simple but as complex as this: The choices we make out of love bring us joy and peace, and the choices we make out of selfishness bring us hardships and suffering.

The most difficult to understand underlying reality of all appearances is our eternal innocence, as many will accept at least the possibility of our original innocence during the process of creating unique souls. However, our eternal innocence is extremely difficult to accept and have knowledge of because it challenges what we believe is the very foundation and meaning of our existence.

We have been conditioned to believe that we are separate from God with a separate personal mind with absolute free will and therefore are blameworthy, culpable, and guilty for our "sins." This worldly idea of having a separate personal mind and absolute free will leads us to believe that every adult must be blameworthy for his or her errors and mistakes in life.

I have heard repeatedly that someone should have known better than to make that mistake or commit that sinful act. Because he should have known better, he must take personal responsibility for his sins. By all appearances, we are blameworthy and, as a result, culpable and guilty, and we must accept full responsibility for our mistakes and sins, but appearances are extremely deceiving. Jesus taught us not to judge by appearances, but we paid little attention to this aspect of his teachings. There is always an underlying reality to all appearances, including sins and evil acts, as appearances are temporal and transient phenomena.

This quote by Fyodor Dostoevsky speaks volumes about the human condition and its lack of understanding concerning the underlying reality of appearances: "Nothing is easier than to denounce the evildoer; nothing is more difficult than to understand him."

There is perfect justice, because without the perfection of karma, souls would never advance in divine love and intelligence. The world cannot always see this justice, as most of the world judges by appearances, and appearances can be very misleading. "What we sow, we reap" was not idle talk by Jesus. Man's attempt at justice is always tainted by inaccuracies and favoritism, but the righteousness of

Divine Love and Intelligence has no errors and shows no favoritism.

What we are learning as expressions of God is to have the ability to respond with love, compassion, and divine intelligence to others and ourselves. Can the reader see the profound but subtle difference between an egocentric act of taking personal responsibility for our mistakes and the idea that we are an expression of Infinite Love and Intelligence learning to have the ability to respond in a loving and intelligence way? The more our will becomes God's will, the greater our ability to respond to others in a loving and compassionate way of being in the world.

16. CAN YOU EXPLAIN THE DIFFERENCE BETWEEN BEING RESPONSIBLE FOR OUR CHOICES AND NOT HAVING PERSONAL RESPONSIBILITY FOR OUR IGNORANCE, WHICH CAUSES US TO ERR?

As humans with eternal souls, we cannot take personal responsibility for our ignorance, but we *appear* to be responsible for our growth and progress toward infinite love and intelligence. This seems quite unfair. Could God have created such an unfair condition for the human soul? This is an extremely difficult concept to understand, but we must learn to view responsibility as the ability to respond rather than us being culpable and therefore blameworthy. Then we might have greater knowledge of the subtle difference between being responsible for our thoughts and actions and our being created with the ability to respond, which is a necessity for creation to occur.

The ability to respond does not mean we must take responsibility for our ignorance, which leads to our mistakes in life. It seems quite unfair that there are consequences for our mistakes due to our ignorance that we cannot take responsibility for due to our original innocence. Those mistakes can and do cause suffering.

How can a God of love and divine intelligence cause its created beings to suffer for their mistakes but hold them responsible for their choices that cause suffering? By asking the question in this section, we are looking through the eyes of a human who feels separate from Infinite Oneness. The effects of inexperience (innocence) are the underlying reality of the mistakes that cause much suffering for the soul.

The following is a truism to reflect on daily: *There is no journey of the soul, and therefore no expression of the Oneness of God without a soul's journey from inexperience to greater and greater awareness.*

There are many synonyms for the word responsible, and the two that come the closest to our being responsible for our thoughts and actions are the concepts of being accountable and answerable, but even being accountable can be thought of as being blameworthy. We must be held accountable and answerable for our actions, but not out of blame; rather, the purpose of accountability is to guide us to greater levels of awareness. If there were no consequences for our thoughts and actions, the soul would not advance in love and intelligence.

Consider the game of chess. The choices we make have consequences, and those consequences teach us to play the game of chess more effectively. Compassion comes to us through our struggles and suffering. When we have suffered enough, we often make a decision to change the choices we make in our lives, and therefore this changes our modes of being in the world.

When we use the analogy of God as a loving parent, we err because, unlike our parents, God is a loving, perfect spirit that has formed the perfect reality of creating and maturing souls. This is the very expression of God, and our taking personal responsibility for our ignorance is in error because it shows that we believe we are separate from God just as we are separate from our parents. No soul is separate from the infinite Source of all that is or ever will be.

Although we appear to have total responsibility for our spiritual growth, the physical and astral worlds are in reality schools of learning. We are not alone in this learning endeavor, but it often feels as though we are. We have universal laws, spiritual guides, spiritual teachers, fate, and, of course, consequences for the choices we make that guide us ever closer to perfect love, compassion, and divine intelligence.

Without our choices and their consequences, we would be androids, mechanical in nature and predictable—not the living, dynamic expressions made in the image of God that we are.

Spiritual wisdom worth remembering: All choices have consequences, because without the notion of reaping what we sow, our souls would not mature and grow in awareness of love and intelligence.

17. WHAT DOES "MADE IN THE IMAGE OF GOD" REALLY MEAN?

We are created with a spark of awareness, which is spirit, because spirit is of God and is the essence of God. This spark of awareness is an ember of light within each soul from this Infinite Awareness that never sleeps and never leaves us. As conscious beings, we learn from our experiences to advance in love and divine intelligence; as our awareness expands, we mature as souls, and this soul growth evolves us into what some call gods. As gods, we have creative power that we can only imagine at this level of our consciousness development.

This spiritual ember/spark of light whispers perfect love and intelligence to us, and with enough experiences and time, we listen and awaken to our true reality as divine expressions of That That Is. With this ember/spark of light, as well as with enough experiences and time, our original innocence is transformed into the perfection of spiritual wisdom.

This spark of awareness within us gives us a longing to be like our creator. Another term for this longing is desire, but often it is misguided desire due to our limited awareness that we err and commit evil acts of violence on others and ourselves. This longing for greater awareness is the journey of the soul.

We as souls are a manifestation of That That Is; we are not separate beings. By all appearances, we should be taking individual responsibility for our errors, and our suffering is the punishment for making those mistakes that most call sin. Appearances are very deceiving and unreliable.

The consequences for the choices we make in life guide us to greater degrees of love and divine intelligence. Consequences for our choices and actions are one of the greatest of spiritual laws: We reap what we sow. This profound spiritual principle is like a cosmic mirror that guides us in our ability to respond with greater compassion to others and ourselves.

Literally, we are gods in the making, and with almost infinite experiences of suffering, joy, and wisdom, we as souls can evolve to what many refer to as Christ

Consciousness. Much of our suffering stems from our choices we make that are not in alignment with love and divine intelligence. The rest of our suffering comes to us because we are created as unique souls by an evolution-of-consciousness process by living in a harsh, physical world.

It is the variation of our suffering and the friction of life that creates every soul as unique and awakens the soul with the ability to respond to self and others with compassion, unconditional love, and divine intelligence. Ask yourself how effective the evolution-of-consciousness process would be without struggles, adversities, and suffering. Many of our struggles in life send us a message that if our thoughts and actions are not in alignment with love and divine intelligence, we can suffer. You have probably known many people who have lived a selfish and materialistic life until their suffering became so great that they sought a higher purpose and meaning to their lives.

My own life is a living example of this phenomenon of suffering and happiness, as it took forty-nine years before I began my spiritual search for purpose and meaning that lay beyond self-centeredness and materialism. I had thought deeply about the mysteries of life for much of my life, but did not begin in earnest my own spiritual search until almost fifty years of age. Those problems we experience in our lives that we so despise and that come to us in life are not random events, nor are they punishments; they come to us to awaken us to our reality of being expressions of God.

The problems that cause much of our suffering have spiritual meanings, and they compel us to move beyond our denial as victims and to examine our existing mode of being in this world. This examination is what I refer to as our dark night of the soul. A thirteenth century Sufi poet and mystic named Rumi said, "Yesterday I was clever, so

I wanted to change the world. Today I am wise, so I am changing myself."

Usually, a significant emotional event in our lives gives us a wake-up call. We're shown that we need to change ourselves and not spend our lives in denial, and we begin to see the fallacy of believing that by changing others we can find happiness and peace of mind. It is irrational to think we can change others while we remain our selfish selves, but this behavior has its home in ignorance, and of course, that ignorance has its origin in our original and therefore eternal innocence within the perfection of Perfect Awareness.

It is very painful to look into the mirror and see ourselves for who we really are. The initial mental suffering may be great, but the benefits will be greater if we are able to commit to being expressions of Ultimate Reality and give up the erroneous idea that we are separate beings who have fallen from the grace of God. How can we fall or separate from God? We are expressions of an Absolute Oneness without boundaries. Would a God of infinite love and divine intelligence reject its own creation?

Our problems do not end after we have looked into the proverbial mirror; often our problems and suffering intensify, especially if we judge ourselves too harshly and fail to see that we cannot take individual responsibility for our ignorance. This acceptance is extremely difficult to do, as our egos will not give up the idea that they are separate entities. This belief in being a separate entity promotes a sense of guilt when mistakes are made, and this self-guilt confirms the ego's sense of being separate from others and God.

18. WHY SHOULD WE NOT FEEL GUILTY FOR OUR ERRORS AND MISTAKES?

We should not feel guilty because this hides the true meaning of our sins and errors. The underlying reality of our sins and negative actions is ignorance. This ignorance has its home in our original innocence because we did not create the process that created every soul with limited awareness. With time, life experience and karma make every soul a unique soul. How can we feel guilty for our ignorance if we did not create it? The ego often wallows in guilt, as doing so is self-confirming that the ego is a separate entity from its Creator.

Proof of the ego's desire to feel guilty is the popularity of religious institutions that teach the need to feel guilt for our sins. Many followers will give huge sums of money to try to get rid of that self-confirming guilt. These religious institutions are needed and must not be condemned, as they are often representative of the beginning stages of our evolution-of-consciousness process in this life, in past lives, or in future lives.

Jesus saw the underlying reality of ignorance as innocence. When a crowd of people had gathered to stone to death a woman accused of adultery, he asked those without sin to cast the first stone, and everyone walked away. Then Jesus told the woman, "Neither do I condemn thee. Go and sin no more" (John 8:11, KJV Bible). The same divine intelligence existed when Jesus stated, "Love your enemies" (Matthew 5:44, Luke 6:27, KJV Bible), for how can we love our enemies if we believe them to be culpable, blameworthy, and even evil and we are unable to see not only their original innocence, but their eternal innocence?

Because we have been created with the ability to respond within the infinite oneness of God, every response creates karma, which Jesus spoke of as "what we sow, we reap." Every thought, choice, action, or reaction that is not in alignment with this infinite Oneness of perfect love and intelligence has consequences that can cause us some level of suffering.

Likewise, every thought, choice, action, or reaction that is in alignment with love and divine intelligence has consequences that reveal to us levels of peace, joyfulness, and bliss.

The evolution-of-consciousness process demands that our responses have consequences to advance our souls in love and divine intelligence. These consequences are often labeled as both positive and negative experiences, and these temporal phenomena advance our souls ever closer to the infinite awareness of God.

Our successes and failures have the potential to teach us profound lessons in life. As we advance in our ability to respond to phenomena with righteous judgment, we see our misguided desires that we label as sin and evil not as failures, but as lessons, which are often severe lessons in life that advance the soul. Without the universal principle of what we sow, we reap, the evolution-of-consciousness process would not be a progression, but a static existence for the expressions of God we call souls. With each choice we make there is an opportunity for a learning experience to advance our soul, in our awareness of our divine reality.

If we were not eternally innocent at the very core of our being, which is spirit, then there would have to be an aspect or fragment of God that is not innocent and therefore not pure and perfect love. How can our eternal innocence be a reality and not just wishful or foolish thinking? Because we are unique expressions of this Oneness most call God, and this Oneness is infinite All and All.

It feels like and looks like we are separate from God, even children of God, but this analogy of being a child of God fails to understand that God is Infinite Oneness. Referring to ourselves as children of God is still making God in our human image. The fragile and fearful ego thrives by making God in its image.

As expressions of God, we have been created with a perception of other. This reveals itself as being separate from God. This is an extremely powerful perception because it has deceived the most preeminent religious and atheist intellectuals of the world for centuries. It is interesting to note that this perception of being separate from God has not deceived the mystics. Once we understand that sin and evil have their homes in ignorance, and that this ignorance came from our original innocence, then we understand that all of our mistakes and errors in our journey as souls have their origins in our original innocence. Our sins and evil actions are temporal and transient phenomena, not Absolute or Divine Reality.

Phenomena are appearances of an underlying reality, meaning these phenomena are not permanent but temporal. As stated earlier, this is why many Eastern religions call what we perceive as material reality an illusion. This is not quite correct, as the phenomena that occur in our lives and all around us are temporal, transient, and impermanent. We are expressions of God, not illusions, and to call a soul or even a human an illusion is a heresy against oneself and against God. The illusion is to believe that we are a separate being from God and have a separate personal mind.

As aspects of God, we are neither illusions nor separate entities from the mind of God, contrary to what some people in the world will tell you. An illusion is a figment of our imagination. A phenomenon exists, but it is temporal and impermanent; therefore, it is not an illusion. A better term to define the relative-phenomenal world of experiences is transient. Some synonyms for transient are as follows: fleeting, passing, brief, temporary, short lived, momentary, and ephemeral.

It is our created desire and belief that we are separate from our Creator that causes us to feel blameworthy. This creative process of involution, where oneness becomes many souls, makes us feel separate from our Creator and causes us to want to take personal responsibility for our sins and evil actions. We are created with limited awareness, which leads to a perception of believing we are separate from God and have total free will in spite of our ignorance.

This perception of separateness makes it almost impossible to comprehend our eternal innocence. To accept the possible reality of our eternal innocence we must admit to our ignorance and see the fallacy of our belief in free will as an absolute not to be questioned. We would much rather admit to being sinners or victims than be called ignorant or admit to our ignorance.

Our very uniqueness as souls is possible because of our unique experiences, as every experience from the initial spark of awareness of spirit to a soul with a unique persona requires that we feel and act separately from our Creator. The more we advance in awareness of our reality as expressions of God, the more advanced we become as an expression of God's perfect love and divine intelligence. As we advance in awareness of our reality, God's thoughts of infinite, unconditional love and divine intelligence flow though our consciousness like a beautiful mountain stream of clear, pure water. Jesus correctly stated that it was not his will, but God's will, that must be done, and Jesus did not hesitate to give God recognition for the miracles that he performed.

Please do not confuse our eternal innocence with a lack of consequences for our choices or actions that lead to our suffering. Our choices can and do bring hardships and suffering into our lives. Of course, let us not forget that our choices can also bring joy and bliss. The ego despises the reality that all souls at their very core are innocent, because the ego wants to judge everyone, including itself, as good or bad. This judgment process reinforces its beliefs that it is separate, special, and better than most others.

Even the atheist who refuses to believe in a Supreme Being has an ego that wants to be special by maintaining that he or she has no creator. The atheist considers his or her ego personality his or her ultimate reality. It is very egotistical and ignorant to believe that the human ego is our ultimate reality. Nothing upsets the human ego more than being called ignorant. As stated earlier, we humans would much rather be called sinners than be called ignorant.

19. IT SEEMS UNFAIR THAT WE ARE HELD ACCOUNTABLE FOR THE CHOICES WE MAKE IN LIFE, EVEN THOUGH WE HAVE BEEN CREATED WITH LIMITED AWARENESS. CAN YOU EXPLAIN THIS FURTHER?

There are three necessities for the creation and the manifestation of unique souls:

One: We must be created with limited awareness; then, with time, experiences, and choices, we become unique souls with an individualized soul persona. This vibrant and dynamic process creates each soul unique.

Two: We must be created with the ability to respond to other souls, to our thoughts, and to the external conditions in life. This ability to respond is the dynamic expression of the Infinite Mind. God experiences its infinite potential through the creation of living souls.

We have been created with more than just the ability to respond; we also have the ability to progress in love and divine intelligence. The combination of these two abilities is God expressing its infinite potential. As souls, we are divine living aspects of God; this is why God sees our innocence where we see sin and evil. As we become more advanced in spiritual discernment, we see the underlying reality of phenomena, such as the misguided desires of sin and evil.

Three: Oneness cannot create anything outside its Infinite Mind; therefore, as souls, we exist within the Mind of Oneness. Without a soul's ability to respond to other souls through the miracle of a life force we know as consciousness, Infinite Mind would be static and be in absolute stillness. Just one look through the Hubble telescope gives us a panoramic view of this vibrant and dynamic reality of God.

If we were created with the perfect awareness that God has, that would be the duplication of the infinite All in All, and infinite by its very definition of being without boundaries cannot be duplicated. Contemplate whether God made every soul perfect and exactly like its Infinite Awareness; that would not be the creation of unique souls but a static stillness of Pure and Perfect Awareness. The uniqueness of each soul responding to other unique souls is the vitality and the dynamic expression of God revealing its infinite potential.

There cannot be two infinites, as this would defy our existing knowledge of infinite. If we see ourselves as being able to be separate from God, then we fail to have understanding of infinite. Infinite means never ending, limitless, and unbounded; therefore, nothing can exist outside of infinite. As living souls, we exist within the infinite oneness of God. We live, and move, and have our being within the infinity of God. For God to express its immeasurable and dynamic potential, it must create souls *within* its infinite All and All.

To be individualized expressions, we must have the ability to express and respond as unique expressions of Oneness. The creation process creates each soul unique, and this uniqueness creates within each soul the ability to respond to other souls. The good news is that as we have these serial experiences in the realm of time that we call life, these experiences advance our souls in love and in a greater awareness of reality. A soul's journey, with its consequences of reaping what it sows, gives the soul a greater ability to respond in love and intelligence.

What feels like punishment is actually a necessity. Granted, it sure does not seem like a necessity of life when we are living through reaping what we have sown. Karma has many faces; not only does it give perfect feedback to create every soul unique, but it is influential in every soul's evolution-of-consciousness process.

We are created as a spark of awareness, best defined as the involution process, and through each soul's almost infinite number of experiences, this spark of awareness expands to a perceived personal mind. This personal mind that we call a soul continues to progress to what some call Christ Consciousness, where our will grows ever closer to God's will. The soul's journey is expression and manifestation of the Infinite Absolute Oneness that most call God expressing its dynamic potential. As our will draws ever closer to God's will, we have truly become more loving and compassionate divine expressions of the Infinite Oneness.

The journey of the soul creates each soul uniquely and is a necessary creative process for God to express its dynamic potential within its own Mind in an infinite variety of unique expressions that we call souls. The infinite and unique expressions of God require that all of creation must not only be relative but also the creation of a phenomenal world. The relative-phenomenal world was created at the very instant that the big bang occurred.

It does seem terribly unfair that we have been created with less than perfect knowledge and understanding until we reach that level of knowledge that we see with clarity that we owe our ability to respond to others and our ability to have a relationship with another soul to the Divine Mind (God). God as Infinite Oneness expresses its infinite potential within its own Divine Mind; therefore, we are indeed made in the image of God.

Because of the necessity for Oneness to become many, we must be created with less than the perfect awareness of our Creator. This necessity to create souls with less than perfect awareness is our original innocence. Our eternal innocence is that we live, and move, and have our being within the Divine Mind.

20. WHAT IS ENLIGHTENMENT, AND WHY IS IT SO DIFFICULT TO ATTAIN?

Enlightenment comes in the realization of a spiritual truth and advances that soul's awareness of reality from being ego-centered to being God-centered or divine-centered. This is not a God made in the image of man but a God that is infinite love, intelligence, and vitality, and that has the necessity to create and express its dynamic potential. We humans and all of nature are an outcome of God's necessity to create and express its dynamic potential.

One of the highest attainments of enlightenment as a human is the moment when the seeker realizes what can best be described as the self-realization of one's divine oneness with God. We can have knowledge that we are indeed an expression of God, but knowledge is not a realization. Knowledge can be in the realm of the intellect, whereas a realization is in the realm of understanding and divine intelligence.

If anyone claims to be self-realized, but he still considers sin and evil realities of the human experience and not phenomena, he has yet to awaken to his godliness as an expression of God. We must have compassion for those who believe this, as they have succumbed to the needs of their ego, and they feel the brunt of their self-deception every day of their lives. Understanding that sin and evil are rooted in ignorance can be helpful to a soul's journey to a greater awareness of reality.

Enlightenment is easier said than done because living the life of a human, with its system of beliefs, conditions us to believe that we are our body and our thoughts. It is nearly impossible to overcome our conditioned beliefs and see our true reality as eternal souls. Some people will try to convince you that they know they are eternal souls, but their knowing is usually based on beliefs, not on a realization. There is a monumental difference between a knowing based on beliefs and a knowing beyond knowing based upon a realization.

The ego loves many things, with free will being the most popular among them. For many who are considered new-thought seekers, attaining enlightenment is a very popular belief and an especially sought-after goal. Both the belief in free will and the belief that we have the ability to attain enlightenment through effort alone are based in unawareness and not intelligence.

I assure you that when humans cross over to the other side, they experience the reality that they are eternal and that the earth experience is only a temporal drama to progress their souls. It is true that as the human race becomes more intelligent, a greater number of humans will attain greater awareness, but enlightenment is but one phase on our long evolutionary journey as a soul. We are gods in the making; so don't be misled into thinking that enlightenment is near the end of our journey to perfect awareness.

We cannot teach our understanding of a truth to others because truth comes to us by the path of revelation followed by an instant realization, and not by a process of learning and attaining knowledge. This is why such advanced souls as Jesus and Buddha had limited success in teaching others their understanding of a truth or truths. Two examples of spiritual truths are to love your enemies and to have compassion for all. How many of us can truly say that we love our enemies and have compassion for all?

I find it interesting that people who have attained an enlightened status spend most of their lives attempting to teach others how to achieve enlightenment. Attaining an enlightened moment that we are eternal souls during our incarnation as a human eliminates much of our suffering, because we have removed ourselves from the drama and attachment of human life as our only existence.

It is difficult to attain enlightenment because of the grasp that our ego, society, conditioned beliefs, and paradigms have on our consciousness. Again, we learn to believe that we are our thoughts and our body. Our mind can be perceived as our worst enemy because of the suffering it brings us, but within that suffering, opportunities arise to acquire a realization of a truth. Suffering can lead to extreme frustration, and this mental turmoil can cause the ego to surrender its hold on our consciousness. This inner turmoil can often lead to surrender, which can open our mind for a revelation to occur.

This path to the surrender of the ego I experienced early in my spiritual seeking when I threw both arms up in the air on a mountaintop near Superior, Arizona and asked, "What am I missing?" I heard a voice a few feet above me say, "Just about everything." This was a defining moment in my life—the kind I would never forget. Experiences such as these offer great opportunities for change.

21. HOW CAN FAILURE DEVELOP OUR SOUL?

Persevering when life gives us failures allows those failures to have the opportunity to develop our soul. Think about your own life. What experiences taught you the most about yourself and the world? Without our perceived failures and successes, what would be the purpose of living a physical life on earth?

The reality of life is this: failure is an illusion. There is no such thing as a spiritual failure, because if we did not need to try and possibly fail, we would not have failed. Where others see failure, the soul sees opportunities. This was one of the hardest concepts I taught when I was an organizational consultant. Continuous improvement teams always wanted to write problem statements, but I asked them instead to write opportunity statements. A problem is an opportunity; likewise, a failure is a lesson in life. When failure comes into our lives, the choices we make decide our destiny and our karma.

As stated earlier in this book, human life is like a lapidary machine that polishes rocks to reveal their beauty. Each hour inside the lapidary machine is like one incarnation as a human experiencing the drama of human life. The drama of rejection, loneliness, grief, and failure that is created in our lives is like the rotation of the lapidary machine, which creates friction on the surface of the rocks. The polishing effect reveals the rocks' true beauty; likewise, the effect of physical life on a soul's consciousness reveals a greater reflection of Perfect Awareness. This advancement in awareness draws us closer to God because our consciousness becomes increasingly more in union with our spirit.

It is important to realize that human life does not make us a perfect reflection of God. Once we graduate from life on earth, we still have a very long, if not eternal journey ahead of us. We can become spiritual guides, healer souls, and spiritual teachers, then masters that teach guides, healers, and teachers. As it is the soul's destiny to advance, our soul becomes an elder soul that mentors master souls.

Every soul's journey resembles a pyramid. As a soul evolves in its awareness of reality, it climbs the steps of this divine pyramid evolving ever closer to the Oneness at the peak of the pyramid. Please don't confuse the analogy of a divine pyramid with the term pyramid scheme. A pyramid scheme is an example of a human's limited awareness and misguided desire to convince others to participate in an ill-advised deception that offers riches for little effort and money. Nothing escapes karma, not only for those who create the pyramid scheme, but also to a lesser degree for those who participate in their misguided desire to attain riches through the deception of others.

Beyond self-realization, we journey as a soul toward the top of the pyramid and becoming co-creators with God on a cosmic scale. It may be possible for some souls to create planets with life on them. The reality of soul evolution is that we draw ever closer to infinite perfection and awareness. When a soul reaches the peak of this divine ladder of spiritual reality, that soul has attained a level of cosmic consciousness to access the vitality and creative abilities needed to be a co-creator on a cosmic scale.

The spirit within each soul assures that the soul has the desire to seek perfection. There are no exceptions. Those who teach or believe that we are children of God and not expressions within the oneness of God have yet to understand the relationship of spirit, soul, and ego.

22. WHY DOES THE EARTH EXPERIENCE OFFER MORE OPPORTUNITIES TO ADVANCE THE SOUL THAN THE ASTRAL WORLD PROVIDES?

The mature soul understands that human life is a short, temporal experience and is willing to struggle and even suffer to grow in intelligence. Our attachments, cravings, physical desires, and also our life's joys and challenges can create an environment that is conducive to our awakening to the spirit within.

The variation that exists in this physical relative-phenomenal world provides each soul tremendous opportunities to respond with compassion for all and to seek divine intelligence. Variation is the stuff of life; the more variation we experience, the greater our opportunities to learn love, compassion, and divine intelligence.

Recently I was watching a movie with a friend; after the movie, I asked what she thought of the quality of acting by the actress, and she responded, "She was a so-so actress." I was devastated because I thought the actress was wonderful, even deserving of an Academy Award. I walked out into my yard and wondered why it was such a downer that my friend did not agree with my observation of this actress's performance. After some reflection, I realized that we want others to believe what we believe, and then, with further thought, I realized my friend has had entirely different life experiences than I.

One of my significant life experiences and memories with a loved one was similar to the plot of the movie. Even though I experienced it many decades earlier, those memories are with me to this day. This similarly of experiences caused me to view the movie with an entirely different frame of reference and set of eyes.

My point for revealing this story is that every experience is different for every soul. What my friend saw as so-so acting, I saw as a deep emotional drama that the actress portrayed beautifully and that reflected some of my own past emotional experiences and existing memories. This same movie affected both my friend and I differently due to our experiences in life. This is an example of how such experiences over time make every soul unique.

There is a popular expression that we learn light by experiencing darkness. Translated, this means we learn intelligence by experiencing ignorance. Human life gives a soul the opportunity to use intelligence, creativity, and our soul's inner desire for perfection to triumph over adversity. Those who state that desire is the root cause of our suffering fail to see how the spirit within us fuels our desire (longing) for perfect love and divine intelligence. It is misplaced or misguided desire that is often the root cause of our suffering.

Desire is not the culprit; ignorance is. All misplaced or misguided desire has its origin in ignorance. All creativity must have a beginning as unawareness. It is interesting to note that without some degree or level of ignorance, there can be no individualized creation of others who can experience joys, discoveries, relationships, and love.

That joy of discovery can be something as simple yet profound as working with preschool children to help them learn how to print a letter of the alphabet; the joy they express in their eyes and the smile that comes to their face is not only for them but also for the teacher. A joy shared is one of the divine moments of a relationship between teacher and student. That joy has its origin in our original innocence.

This earthly experience gives every soul a variety of experiences. Whether that soul is the teacher or the student, the variety of knowledge and experiences is the stuff of life. In the world of consulting, process improvement "experts" teach that variation is the enemy. Undesirable variation is indeed very troublesome because it creates defects and chaos, but they err in their conclusion that we must treat variation as the enemy. The underlying reality of all variation is some degree of a soul's unawareness of its perfect reality that we call spirit. Always keep in mind that a synonym for unawareness is ignorance.

The reality is that variation in a relative-phenomenal world gives us perfect feedback, which can guide us to perfection. I hope one can see the analogy here between desire and variation. Desire is our intrinsic nature as a soul to seek intelligence and love driven by spirit. Likewise, variation is the stuff of life that makes every soul unique; without variation there is no unique consciousness or perception of other. From the soul's perspective, Earth is a schoolroom. The harshness and joys of life on Earth give the soul an opportunity to participate in the colossal drama of human life with its abundance of desire and variation.

Because the human ego sees human life as its one and only reality, this adds intensity and a perception of finality to our lives. Proof of this can be seen in the immense amount of money spent to keep us alive, sometimes even in a coma state, because our perception of human life is that when we die we cease to exist.

When our loved ones die, we experience grief, so we try to keep them here with us for as long as possible, and often at great expense. It is interesting to note that our loved ones who have crossed over do not want us to grieve for them, as it often holds them back in their journey into these astral worlds of paradise.

Our eternal reality resides within our soul, not our human ego. The human ego lives in fear of losing its identity, whereas when a more advanced soul reincarnates, it obtains a human identity to participate in this temporal realism called life on Earth. This temporal reality as a human offers tremendous opportunities to advance in love and divine intelligence.

The time will come in human evolution when knowledge about the origin of suffering, the origin of ignorance, and the meaning and purpose of creation will cause humans to focus more on their soul development than worldly success. Instead of believing that we have one life to live, maybe we will understand that we live one life at a time.

Religion is our existing system of beliefs that focuses on our soul, but religious beliefs still give God human traits. Trying to please a deity that has been given human traits is impossible and creates endless conflict and suffering in the world. This condition will not always exist in the world, because acquiring unconditional love and divine intelligence is an evolutionary upward spiral for our eternal souls and for the entire human species. This evolutionary upward spiral is the progression of the soul that some refer to as the law of progression or the law of progress.

23. PLEASE EXPLAIN THE EVOLUTION OF THE SOUL IN MORE DETAIL.

A soul is created with original innocence, which means it has been created with a consciousness that has less than perfect intelligence. Maybe less is not the right word to use. Perhaps it would be better to think of a soul as an aspect or fragment of the infinite awareness and essence of God. Because a soul is created with a consciousness that has limited awareness, it is unaware of its inner perfection. An important reality of creation is that *every soul's created limited awareness creates an awareness of other.*

Soul evolution is an evolution-of-consciousness process toward infinite awareness. If a soul were capable of attaining infinite awareness in the moment of its creation, that soul's individualized identity would cease to exist. The loss of personal identity frightens the human ego-centered mind because we humans fail to see the bliss and perfection of progressing in the awareness of self as a divine being.

It is good to keep in mind that even if a soul can indeed attain a status of infinite awareness, we never lose our identity because our identity becomes That That Is. Much of my research has revealed that we keep our uniqueness as a soul but we draw ever closer to the infinite awareness of God. Infinite awareness may be just that: a never-ending progression of the soul.

I have read that God is good at creating a great mystery because it has hidden its very essence within us. We spend our lives looking outside ourselves for answers, but due to our innocence, we fail to see the divine reality within us, which is spirit.

The journey toward Oneness is a progression toward perfect intelligence and awakening to this divine reality within our soul called spirit. Soul evolution is a dynamic upward-spiral progression toward perfection. In our soul's evolutionary journey, we experience human life, other dimensions, being a spiritual guide, teacher, advisor, or master, and being a god with a small *g*. As a god, our soul becomes a co-creator with God, but always within the boundaries of God. As the soul evolves to a godlike status in divine intelligence, it may attain enough power to create planets, galaxies, and life forces that exist on planets such as Earth. We know these life forces as nature.

24. YOU SAY OUR SOULS BECOME LIKE GODS AND CO-CREATORS WITH GOD. AREN'T THESE EGOTISTICAL BELIEFS?

Many people will shudder at what I have just stated, because we have been conditioned to believe that we are inferior or worse, that we are sinners and therefore separate from God. Actually, it is very egocentric to believe that we can fall from the grace of God. The very definition of God is perfection and infinite grace. How can anyone fall from infinite grace?

Do not underestimate the ego. It lives in fear and can be very deceptive, so it tries in vain to believe that it is in control of its destiny. The fear of death keeps the ego in a constant state of wanting and not wanting to validate itself as a reality and to feel special.

Soul evolution is about continual improvement and progression in love and divine intelligence. With the ongoing progression in divine intelligence comes a greater power to create. This is a divine purpose, because with power there must be intelligence. History has given us many examples of individuals and nations that have been given great power, but have not used that power with love and intelligence. Progressing from a beginner soul to a co-creator with God is the reality of soul evolution. Anyone who attains knowledge of the origin of ignorance and its correlation to soul evolution gains valuable insights into the meaning and purpose of creation.

25. HOW DOES UNDERSTANDING THE ORIGIN OF IGNORANCE GIVE US INSIGHTS INTO THE MEANING OF CREATION?

Attaining knowledge or an understanding of the origin of ignorance draws us closer to the creative process of involution of awareness and evolution-of-consciousness progression for each unique soul. When we have knowledge or understanding of the origin of ignorance, we see more clearly that the Creator must create us with an innocence of our oneness with others so that we can have a perception of other.

The oneness of God becomes the many expressions of its Godself by the creation of inexperienced souls that lack perfect love and divine intelligence. When this created innocent soul seeks divine wisdom, it reveals its lack of knowing. This lack of knowing is called ignorance. As we gain knowledge of the origin of ignorance, we see with greater clarity the attributes and causal correlation of perfection, the infinite, and oneness.

26. WHAT HAPPENS IF WE DON'T HAVE AN UNDERSTANDING OF THE ORIGIN OF IGNORANCE?

A whole host of difficulties arises in the world because of our lack of understanding that the origin of ignorance is our original and eternal innocence. Some believe that human life is nothing but suffering, and should be avoided at all costs. I read in a religious book that this world is disgusting and worthless. This statement does not stand up to the logic or reasoning of an intelligent universe. Perfect Intelligence does not create worthless worlds or beings, but it does create inexperienced souls that err in their ability to respond consistently with love and intelligence to life's challenges.

The world seems insane when we judge it by appearances. For instance, humans killed more than one hundred million of their own species in the twentieth century. Does not that have the appearance of insanity? The reality is that when we understand the origin of ignorance, we observe with clarity that the root cause of that appearance of insanity was ignorance. We also can see that ignorance has its home in the inability of the soul to make valid and loving choices due to its inexperience.

Innocence is blamelessness and purity, and that purity is the very essence within every soul, which is spirit. It is an enormous paradigm shift for anyone to comprehend that innocence and killing are interrelated by ignorance. Even self-proclaimed enlightened individuals fail to see the relationship of innocence and ignorance.

Given time and experiences, with the perfection of karma, each soul will see that the underlying reality of ignorance is our eternal innocence. That essence within us called spirit is our eternal innocence. The enlightened human view of suffering is ignorance. The souls that have advanced in awareness to godlike status see the innocence of spirit even when they are being harmed by others.

27.   I AM STILL CONFUSED. CAN YOU GIVE ME MORE EXAMPLES EXPLAINING WHY ANYONE NEEDS TO KNOW ABOUT THE ORIGIN OF IGNORANCE?

Another difficulty that arises if we do not have knowledge or understanding about the origin of ignorance is that we give God human traits, such as the need to judge and punish. This creates a lot of suffering in the world. When the terrorists flew into the World Trade Center on September 11, 2001, they yelled, "God is great." This is an example of a form of hatred, which always has its root in ignorance, being played out on the world scene. They lacked divine intelligence, but then we all lack some level of perfect intelligence.

We called the terrorists evil rather than see the cause of their hatred and evil acts, which was ignorance. Labeling someone evil hides the root cause or origin of his actions and causes us to blame and judge him. We create suffering for ourselves when we blame and judge others. We are all connected to this universal Oneness, so what we do to others, we do to ourselves. Labeling anyone evil prevents us from looking inside our own consciousness and recognizing that our need to judge and blame others is based in our own unawareness of our divine reality.

Our labeling anyone evil, including nations, prevents us from understanding that the underlying reality of their evil deeds is ignorance. Evil reveals itself as phenomena that we experience, and the underlying reality of phenomena and experiences is consciousness. Those invalid thoughts in consciousness that cause evil have their home in our not yet realizing the truth of our oneness with God. This level of realization sees the futility in misguided desires such as greed, selfishness, and the desire to harm others.

Every Christian knows that Jesus taught us to love our enemies, and Jesus actually loved his enemies. Knowing we should love our enemies is exponentially different from loving our enemies. One is based in knowing that we should love our enemies and the other is based in knowing beyond knowing the divine essence in every living soul.

What is the origin of that ignorance? It is in the process that creates each soul with unawareness and thus an innocence of his or her perfect reality.

28. YOUR STATEMENTS APPEAR TO BE SUGGESTING THAT INNOCENCE AND HARMING OTHERS ARE RELATED. WOULD YOU EXPLAIN THE RELATIONSHIP BETWEEN INNOCENCE AND HARMING OTHERS?

All of God's creation is innocent, because God cannot create a consciousness with a perception of other without innocence. Souls are innocent of their reality because they have been created to be individualized life forces, and this prevents them from seeing that they are manifestations and ongoing eternal expressions of Oneness. We know this created conscious life force as a soul. For God to manifest others, express its potential, and experience its dynamic creative perfection in unique ways, every soul must be created innocent of its divine reality.

A daily reflection: There is no journey of the soul or expression of God without every soul being created with original innocence.

An innocent soul reveals its ignorance when it seeks to be like its creator. This desire to seek perfection comes from the spirit whispering perfection to our soul. As our soul matures, the spirit guides our soul. The spirit is the life force and sustaining vitality (energy) for all that exists in the universe, whereas individualized consciousness is our created perception of reality.

Harming others for whatever reason is an outcome of ignorance, and that ignorance has its original home in innocence. The understanding of the origin of ignorance reveals the relationship between creation, innocence, ignorance, and suffering.

29. IT IS DIFFICULT FOR ME TO BELIEVE THAT HARMING SOMEONE CAN BE DUE TO INNOCENCE AND NOT EVIL.

The ego loves to judge and condemn others because it suffers from a lack of self-esteem that has manifested in its life's journey from a spark of awareness to a godlike status. This low self-esteem, even to the point of self-hate, has its origin in the soul's original innocence that has manifested as ignorance. The human ego lives in constant fear and denial, and the root cause of that fear is ignorance. Harming, even killing someone, may be judged as an evil act, but that evil act has its home in not knowing that which is available to be known, and is an outcome of our soul's created innocence.

> *"Fear always springs from ignorance."*
> —Ralph Waldo Emerson

Adults may know good behavior from bad, but an immature ego can succumb to anger, jealously, revenge, misguided desires, and selfish behaviors. The world judges by appearances, but the ability to discern the underlying reality of appearances comes with personal experiences, time, and often the harsh feedback of karma. It is exponentially easier to judge others as sinful or evil than to see each soul expressing the purity of the spirit within and longing for understanding.

Our lack of self-esteem keeps us in a constant state of denial of our ignorance. That denial brings a massive amount of suffering into our lives before we figuratively and often literally are brought to our knees. From my point of view, this dark night of the soul is not the end of our suffering because our mental suffering increases before it finds peace.

This constant state of denial can bring such suffering into our lives that we are willing to look into a mirror and see our ignorance up front and personal. It is not pleasant, but it is necessary if we are to become sincere spiritual seekers. We are not victims of ignorance, but expressions of Oneness. We do indeed suffer from our ignorance, but that suffering is the guiding force of karma to expand and develop our soul in love and divine intelligence.

Nothing that God has ever created is evil, but it is possible for God's creation to commit evil acts. I know that sounds like a contradiction, but evil acts are misguided and invalid desires in our attempt to please our human consciousness, which is controlled by our ego. An ego often has succumbed to worldly and impermanent attachments and cravings. This intrinsic desire is an inner longing toward perfection and is the gap between the intelligence of our consciousness and the perfection of our spirit.

Most of the religious world sees desire as the cause of suffering, but it is not; rather, desire that is off target and misguided causes our suffering. An example of this misplaced desire is when a person believes that temporal physical pleasures or successes will give him or her continual happiness. Another example is the belief that we will be happy if we can find the right person to love us.

Often we spend our lives seeking that one right person to make us happy. Continual happiness is an oxymoron. What brings us inner peace is not external but is contained within us, and it is spirit. As we begin to awaken to our spiritual reality and acquire divine intelligence, we become more in alignment with our spirit and attain greater degrees of inner peace.

30. PLEASE EXPLAIN IN SIMPLE TERMS THE DIFFERENCE BETWEEN INNOCENCE AND IGNORANCE.

Ignorance is nothing more than unawareness, and that unawareness arises from our created original innocence. Our original innocence is our eternal innocence simply because we were created as expressions with divine potential to be gods. We did not create our own souls; how can we have personal responsibility for our innocence that manifests itself with the choices we make as our ignorance? At the core of our being and our true reality is Spirit, which is always pure, virtuous, and innocent. This is our eternal innocence and the reality of our spirit within, hidden from our view so that God can manifest itself in infinite and unique expressions of its Oneness. Without our innocence, creation would be a duplication of Infinite Oneness, and it is impossible to duplicate the infinite.

An example of humankind's lack of understanding of infinite is the question, "If God created souls, then who created God?" Infinite has no creator, as infinite has no beginning and no ending. Our finite minds can begin to grasp the concept of unending, but our minds appear to be unable to grasp the concept of no beginning. With God's reality there is no first cause; there is just Isness. The relative-phenomenal world gives us causes and effects; we find the idea of no first cause and no beginning impossible to comprehend.

Our innocence is evidenced by our lack of perfect understanding (wisdom) of the spiritual meaning of what we have been taught to do or not to do. Teaching is not understanding; it is the sharing of knowledge about something. Misguided, selfish desires and ego-centered, self-confirming ideas can overwhelm what we have been taught, but only if we lack understanding. The profound difference between knowing and understanding must be grasped if one is to comprehend the underlying reality of ignorance.

Our ignorance is revealed when we are told not to do something, and we do it anyway despite what we have been taught. Misguided desires can overwhelm being told not to do something in a heartbeat. A misguided desire to gossip about another person cannot exist if we have an understanding that gossip is in the realm of our own low self-esteem and lack of love for self and others. Being told not to gossip is in the realm of knowledge about gossiping, and knowledge pales in comparison to having compassion for self and others.

Compassion is our understanding of the underlying reality of ignorance, which is innocence. Knowledge is like advice; it is still in the realm of a certain level of unawareness that can be overwhelmed by self-centered desires. We see the drama of these self-centered desires playing out every day of our lives in others, and if we are honest, we see it in our own lives. If we are to love our enemies, we must not only have understanding of their original innocence, but their eternal innocence.

Each soul is created unique by a process of experiences, soul choices, and karma. The creation of each unique soul starts with an involution of awareness-consciousness process. This involution process is from the perfect awareness of the Absolute to every soul's limited awareness of their spirit within, which begins each soul's journey toward infinite awareness.

The relative-phenomenal universe reveals itself as thoughts (thoughts are energy). As souls, we perceive those thoughts flowing through our minds. This flow of thoughts is what we refer to as consciousness. Adam and Eve lacked understanding (wisdom), so they did something in spite of being told not to: they ate from the tree of wisdom, which is a metaphor for the tree of the knowledge of good and evil.

We may have been taught not to steal from others, but we may make a choice to steal something that we really thought we needed to make us happy. Most people would call this sin because we know not to steal, but this is actually an example of ignorance. After all, we have been told not to steal, but we have not yet learned the spiritual implications of stealing from others. Our selfish, misguided desires that have their home in ignorance have overwhelmed our being taught not to steal.

Where did that ignorance originate? The valid answer to that question will reveal to the seeker that ignorance, or unawareness, originated in the process that creates unique but imperfect souls. Our original innocence is also our eternal innocence in the eyes of an all-knowing Creator. Shall we trust the eyes of God or our own eyes? The answer to that question is obvious, of course: We should trust the eyes of the infinite perfection of God.

What we *should* have known or not known is not understanding or divine intelligence, contrary to what the world teaches. Another term for understanding is spiritual discernment or spiritual awakening. Adam and Eve, by eating from the tree of the knowledge (wisdom, life), started their journey into spiritual discernment. As the wise serpent told them, from that moment on they would be as gods, knowing (understanding) good from evil.

Teaching or telling someone what to do or not do does not teach understanding; it only teaches him or her to *know* about something. Understanding comes to us through inner realizations by a process of awakening to the reality of a truth.

The *creation* of unique souls creates our *original innocence*; therefore, *innocence* precedes *ignorance*, and *ignorance* precedes *suffering*. Our eternal innocence is our lack of understanding of these divine truths whether we know about them or not. In our ignorance, we usually know right from wrong, but we continue to do wrong for a variety of reasons, most of which spring from misguided, selfish desires. Misguided desires can overwhelm what we know concerning right and wrong, but these desires cannot overwhelm an individualized consciousness that has a knowing beyond knowing of its divine reality.

We think that because we feel separate from God, we can exclude ourselves from the reality of these spiritual truths. We do not understand that we are expressions of God; we feel we are separate persons from all others. As expressions of God, anything we do that is not in alignment with love and divine intelligence can have harsh consequences—that is, we will reap what we sow.

The creation story of Adam and Eve reveals that God created them innocent because they did not know death or the difference between good and evil. Like an innocent creature, they did not spend their days thinking about death; therefore, they lived in paradise, like a pet cat or dog. They did not have understanding of good and evil, which is light and darkness. They had to eat from the tree of knowledge or, better, the tree of divine understanding and wisdom. The fruit from this tree of perfect love and divine intelligence is to know light from darkness.

How does perfect love and intelligence see its creation? As long as we continue to make God in our image and consider ourselves as separate children of God rather than expressions of the Oneness of God, we will continue to see others and ourselves as blameworthy and sinful. This self-blame can manifest itself as self-hate. This self-hate can become troublesome when it projects itself outward to the world and causes problems such as racism, wars, genocide, and terrorism.

We humans, with less than perfect understanding of the underlying reality of our own ignorance, see the ignorance in others, not their innocence, and we blame them and ourselves for it. God, in its perfect understanding of the underlying reality of our ignorance, sees our eternal innocence.

My lifelong friend asked the following question after reading the previous sentence in this book before it was published:

"If the worst sinner is innocent in God's eyes, then why is that sinner in darkness and not in heaven?"

This question is at the heart of our ability to understand our original and indeed our eternal innocence. My response to my friend was as follows: Perfection needs no tampering. Advanced spirits see this perfection, but we, with much less awareness, seldom see the perfection of karma. The underlying reality of all sin and evil is ignorance, and the underlying reality of all ignorance is innocence because spirit is always innocent. Our eternal innocence does not guarantee any soul the ability to not experience the consequences of their actions.

At our core, we are the essence of spirit. What we see as appearances are phenomena, not spirit. All phenomena have an underlying reality of spirit. What the world deems sin and evil is nonexistent within the realm of spirit. Both sin and evil are a misapplied longing for the joy and bliss that awaits every soul in these dimensions of light, love, creativity, and intelligence.

The state of mind that would harm another is a dark and gloomy environment that is centered in self-judgment. Harming another intentionally is akin to harming oneself. The person who harms others has some soul searching to do in order to expunge the self-hate that he or she is projecting onto others. There are spiritual guides who will help that soul stop the cycle of the self-inflicted Hades condition. I have found no evidence in my research that there is an eternal hell. I have found much evidence that indeed a temporal Hades condition can exist for a human soul that intentionally harmed others during its lifetime.

The creator is taking full responsibility for our ignorance. This can be known as grace. When we make God in our image, we give God our human traits of blaming and judging others. Righteous judgment is blameless judgment, contrary to what the world teaches. Righteous judgment has compassion for all including our enemies.

31. ARE YOU SAYING THAT THE ROOT CAUSE OF SIN IS ALWAYS OUR ORIGINAL INNOCENCE?

Yes, that is exactly what I am saying. A cause is something that makes another thing happen, while an effect is the result. For example:

Cause: Susan fell down.
Effect: Susan hurt her leg.

According to Aristotle, we cannot have true knowledge of something until we know its cause. Today, many use a problem-solving method called root cause analysis, which strives to solve problems by identifying its root cause. The root cause of all sin and evil is ignorance, and that ignorance has its home in our original innocence. When errors occur, whether in a factory or in one's life, there is always some level of unawareness.

Creation requires unique and imperfect souls that have original innocence. Suffering is then born from the resulting ignorance and unawareness of those souls.

32. WHAT IS THE DIFFERENCE BETWEEN A REVELATION AND A REALIZATION?

A revelation often occurs a moment before a realization occurs. Think of a revelation as opening the mind for the realization of a truth. When we allow our minds to open, the grace of spirit can cause a revelation to occur. This revelation reveals to the humble (meek) open mind a realization. Realization is the understanding of a truth, whereas revelation is the path to realization. The sequence of events is as follows: first a revelation, then a realization, and then a knowing beyond knowing of a truth. There are untold revelations, realizations, and truths before we attain the status of gods. We are truly gods in the making through the process of soul evolution.

My observation has been that the world confuses an insight with a realization. We see the world anew after a realization, but with an insight, we have acquired additional knowledge about a truth. An insight occurs within the existing paradigm; a realization occurs outside the existing paradigm. Insights usually have very little impact on our lives, but a realization changes our views of reality and our lives forever.

A realization is not a choice or decision to change. Our lives are changed after experiencing a realization because we see the world with a new set of eyes, which is a new awareness of the underlying reality of phenomena. I suspect that it might be possible to live many lives before we reach the level of humility (meekness) to acquire a revelation. Jesus taught the very essence of this truth when he taught that the meek shall inherit the earth.

During Jesus's earthly ministry, many religious zealots claimed that the messiah would rid Israel of Roman domination. One self-proclaimed messiah had a following that accomplished this very goal for a few short years. But the spiritual teachings of Jesus such as love your enemies, the meek shall inherent the earth, and we reap what we sow, have survived the test of time and intelligence.

33. YOU HAVE DESCRIBED THE ORIGIN OF IGNORANCE FOR EACH SOUL. CAN YOU DEFINE THE ORIGIN OF IGNORANCE AS IT APPLIES TO A TIMELESS REALITY?

In a timeless reality, which of course is an infinite reality, there is no origin of anything, including suffering, ignorance, or creation. This creates a fundamental problem for our minds because the relative-phenomenal world gives us a series of experiences that have a perception of time. Our minds cannot comprehend the infinite; we can only become aware of the attributes of this infinite reality. Only the awareness of "now" can realize the timeless reality of God.

By its very definition, infinite has no origin. Infinite only exists in the present now. Because every soul that God creates is unique, we can discuss the origin of suffering, ignorance, and the meaning of creation. If this infinite creation of unique souls did not exist, then we would be unable to discuss the origin of anything.

34. WHY DO YOU BELIEVE THAT NO SIN OR EVIL EXISTS? EVEN JESUS SPOKE ABOUT SIN.

I have read that the original definition of *sin* was *to miss the mark or target*. It was an archery term converted into a religious word. Missing the mark or target is an excellent way to define sin. Evil acts are a demonstration of sin, and sin is a demonstration of ignorance. To carry this logic even further, ignorance is an outcome of innocence, and innocence is a mandatory condition of creation.

Sin and evil acts are phenomena, and phenomena are not the ultimate reality but temporal or transient occurrences. Because we judge by appearance, which is phenomena, this is a very difficult concept for the human mind to comprehend. God's creation is phenomena, and all of creation is relative phenomena. We live in a relative-phenomenal world for a very good reason. This world allows all the unique souls that are living a human experience to perceive one another as separate beings.

It is good to remind ourselves often that we were created with a less than perfect consciousness so that we could have the perception and relationships with others. It is this perception of other that keeps us from seeing our true essence, and that essence is spirit. We were created as innocent souls, and we will always be innocent souls despite what others try to tell us.

No human can be called evil, for to call someone evil is to call the very essence of God evil. Evil is not an absolute; it is the phenomena of ignorance and a temporal reality. Of course, that temporal reality could be a very long time in a human's concept of time. Every soul will awaken to the goodness of God, but the time element for each soul to awaken as an expression of God is relative; some souls take longer than others do. The underlying reality of every evil act is misguided, self-centered desires, and misguided desires have their home in ignorance. This ignorance is the unawareness that our spirit and God's spirit are one.

The most unspeakably evil act we can ever commit cannot harm our spirit, but it can impair our consciousness. This is the reason for healer souls in the astral world. Our own self-judgment as humans and as souls can be very harmful to us. We often need to receive healing from these healer souls when we cross over to another dimension, which is every soul's eternal home.

It is of value to any spiritual seeker to differentiate between consciousness and awareness. Consciousness is that which was created by an evolutionary process of growth in awareness; it is not the ultimate reality and therefore can be contaminated and impaired. The ultimate reality is spirit, and our spirit is beyond any harm or destruction. God is infinite spirit and beyond any impairment or annihilation.

Those who believe in an eternal hell fail to understand that we are a manifestation of this Infinite Oneness. For God to condemn or permit any of its creation to an eternity in hell is to condemn an aspect of itself to hell. An all-knowing, infinite God with perfect intelligence and immaculate love does not make mistakes.

Our very essence as created beings is spirit, and this spirit cannot be harmed, destroyed, or contaminated. Spirit is perfect love, and nothing penetrates it, neither sin nor evil nor ignorance. Our ego in its ignorance will tell us differently, because it has made God in its image. The very idea of an infinite Reality, which has no beginning or ending, is perfection.

35. IS IGNORANCE THE ENEMY?

Many people conclude that ignorance is the enemy, but this is incorrect. Understanding the origin of ignorance reveals to us the necessity of innocence to create a perception of other. Our innocence will always reveal itself as ignorance because of a soul's longing toward the perfection of Oneness. We will all reveal our ignorance and commit sin and evil acts in one or many of our lives as humans.

Trying to evaluate a person by looking at his or her existing life on earth would be the same as conducting a statistical analysis using a sample size of one to make an accurate evaluation of a population. An example of this is like asking one person to define sin and expecting his answer to reflect the rest of the world's definition of sin. Another example would be to measure one person's height in a room of about eighty people and then expect to have everyone in the room be that same height. To understand the origin of ignorance requires a person to understand the necessity of variation and innocence for creation to occur rather than to see ignorance as the enemy.

Innocence does not know that which is available to be known. Ignorance is simply not yet acquiring that which is available to be known to us. We were created innocent of our reality and with limited awareness, so how can we be expected to know all there is to know? If we were created with perfect intelligence, we would only see oneness; we would not have a perception of other. This would not be creation, but duplication, and Infinite Oneness cannot duplicate itself to become many souls. The path to the creation of many unique souls is our original innocence.

36. YOUR STATEMENTS SOUND LIKE THE STORY OF ADAM AND EVE TO ME, AND I WAS TAUGHT THAT THEY COMMITTED A SIN BY EATING FROM THE TREE OF KNOWLEDGE.

"Then the Lord God placed the man in the Garden of Eden to cultivate it and guard it. He told him, 'You may eat the fruit of any tree in the garden, except the tree that gives knowledge of what is good and what is bad.'"
—(Genesis 2:15-17 Good News Bible)

Whoever wrote the Adam and Eve story might have known the origin of suffering and the origin of ignorance. But those who have interpreted this story have lacked sufficient understanding of the origin of suffering and ignorance, so they have misunderstood its divine wisdom. That is the certainty of ignorance; it fails to see the reality of a truth, so it redefines its version of that truth and then teaches a misguided translation of it to the world.

I hope we can see the challenges that lie ahead of us when we try to comprehend the origins of suffering and ignorance, which were described in the story of Adam and Eve thousands of years ago, and we humans still fail to see the significance of it. There was no original sin only original innocence.

37. HOW DOES EATING FROM THE TREE OF THE KNOWLEDGE OF GOOD AND EVIL HAVE ANYTHING TO DO WITH THE ORIGINS OF SUFFERING AND IGNORANCE?

The origin of suffering is the willingness of a soul to become attached to this temporal human body, and this attachment creates a lot of suffering in our lives. Attachment to our physical bodies, of course, is based in ignorance. It is important that we see the difference between a symptom of ignorance, such as attachment and craving, and the origin of suffering, which is ignorance. Confusing a symptom with the origin of anything is a common mistake of humanity. Symptoms are outcomes, whereas an origin is a root cause. Attachments and cravings are the effects of ignorance, not the cause of ignorance.

My consulting experience has taught me that the number one cause of defects and organizational chaos is when organizations confuse a symptom with a root cause. Organizational chaos and defects cause an abundance of stress for workers, managers, and consumers. This stress can lead to resentment, anger, and frustration. These attributes of stress cause both mental misery and physical suffering. The root cause or origin of that misery and suffering is ignorance.

Once a soul seeks divine wisdom driven by the spirit within its essence, then the soul is willing to possess a temporal human body to have the opportunity to acquire intelligence. This previous sentence helps to explain the origin of ignorance. Eve ate fruit from the tree of wisdom, and this explains to the reader a soul's desire to seek wisdom and to progress in love and intelligence in the astral world. The Garden of Eden is paradise in the astral world, and a mature soul leaves this paradise to live the life of a human to advance in love and intelligence. Souls come to earth to learn from both the challenges of hardships and the joys of living in a physical body.

38. WHY DO YOU BELIEVE THAT YOU WERE ABLE TO DISCOVER THE ANSWERS TO THESE THREE PROFOUND QUESTIONS?

I believe that much of what I discovered was due to fate. A revelation came to me that I suspect was some form of grace, and shortly thereafter, my asking for years to be shown the other side and my prayers were answered in a dream state that some call a visitation. I also had a very focused mind with a minimum of established religious or atheist beliefs.

But the reality is that I never would have discovered the origin of ignorance without a realization of something that I call understanding variation in a relative-phenomenal world. Also, my research approach was to read some books many times over to gain the essence and depth of the message from the author. I was discovering that a single reading of most books failed to communicate the entirety of the authors' knowledge of reality.

So, my final analysis is that I was able to discover the answers to these three profound questions because of a sequence of lifelong experiences that came into my life due to fate. A realization on the necessity of variation to create the relative-phenomenal world and that all variation contains some level of imperfections. I experienced a visitation that showed me the intelligence and compassion of the astral world, and I had a tremendous amount of desire to learn driven by a fear of death, and—maybe the most important—a belief that I could solve the mystery about the origin of ignorance. I refused to accept the advice from those who told me that the origin of ignorance was unknowable.

Recently I attended a spiritual study group meeting during which a young lady asked a question about what the other side is like. The facilitator told her that she would have to wait until she crossed over to know what these astral worlds are like. Later I told her not to accept that kind of advice. The person giving that advice assumes that because he or she does not know, then it is unknowable, but that kind of advice hinders our spiritual search to discover these mysteries of life.

39. HOW CAN SPIRITUAL SEEKERS OVERCOME THEIR IGNORANCE?

One: Much ignorance can be overcome by learning through investigation and scrutinizing the process and results of the spiritual seeking of others, which often leads to personal discoveries that might pave the way for a revelation to occur, which leads to the realization of a truth.

Two: As spiritual seekers, we can seek knowledge in a structured learning environment, such as community colleges, colleges, and universities; by researching the history of religions, and by comparing and contrasting different religious beliefs; by looking for common teachings and themes. The Internet offers a plethora of information on spiritual teachings and the experiences of others.

Three: Perhaps the most important way to overcome our ignorance is to meditate, reflect, contemplate, and become aware of our own flow of thoughts to attain insight into our own selfishness, denial, and lack of empathy for others. This discernment helps us to progress in our greater understanding of the underlying reality of phenomena.

Four: Pray, not petitioning prayers of wanting and not wanting, but prayers of surrender of our selfishness so that we may continually learn to be more compassionate expressions of our Creator, which is Infinite Love and Divine Intelligence.

My prayer that I say often is a prayer to better understand reality and to be able to see the divine righteousness and innocence in all others and myself. It is a short prayer, but it reveals my own inner longing to awaken to the reality of the divine essence of vitality and intelligence that permeates the entire universe and beyond.

Five: Find your niche in life that allows you to be an expression of love and intelligence. When you find that niche, your joy received will be tenfold for your efforts in love and divine intelligence. If at first you don't succeed in finding that niche, try again and again, as every soul is unique; therefore, every soul has a special talent to be a valuable and beneficial presence in this world as well as in the other worlds and dimensions we inhabit after we leave this physical world.

My own niche in life after my retirement was to volunteer in a federally funded educational program for four-year-olds who have the unique challenge of living in a low-income family. They taught me much about love and having joyfulness for life every time I worked with them as a volunteer.

THE LAW OF ONENESS

"Quantum physics thus reveals a basic oneness of the universe."
—*Erwin Schrodinger, Physicist*

"God is a circle whose center is everywhere and circumference nowhere."

—Voltaire

The Law of Oneness, considered the first universal law, states that everything that we see around us comes from the same Source. Some refer to this Oneness as God, Love, Energy, Light, One Mind, or Universal Consciousness. It doesn't matter what we choose to call the Isness of All in All. The point is that the world as we know it does not consist of separate things, and we are not separate from one another. We only seem to be.

The Law of Oneness is one of several universal laws, which are the principles that govern the underlying harmony of the universe. Sadly, most people never take the time to develop an understanding of these universal laws. They go through life relying on what they can see and touch on the outside to determine their perception of reality without ever realizing that things are interconnected and made real because of what's occurring on the inside (One Mind).

Considering all the struggles currently going on in this world, it is easy for us to doubt that there is actually a good reason for all the conflict that we see around us. We need to remember that the only way God can create unique souls that are able to interact with one another is by giving us limited awareness of the divine nature of Oneness. We are innocent of this divinity. This created innocence is mandatory for the creation from Oneness to many to occur.

Science has long known the interconnectivity of all things. American-born British quantum physicist David Bohm is well known for his theory of holomovement. As stated on Wikipedia, his theory is based on "the idea that everything is in a state or process of becoming (what he calls the universal flux). For Bohm, wholeness is not a static oneness, but a dynamic wholeness-in-motion in which everything moves together in an interconnected process."

Mind and matter, he believed, are all abstractions from this universal flux. In other words, we and everything else in the universe are all part of this holomovement (Oneness) and are constantly changing and moving. Bohm believed that the universe is a kind of holographic structure, and this holomovement could neither be measured nor defined. In his book *Wholeness and the Implicate Order*, Bohm states the following:

> To emphasize undivided wholeness, we shall say that what 'carries' an implicate order is the holomovement, which is an unbroken and undivided totality. In certain cases, we can abstract particular aspects of the holomovement (e.g., light, electrons, sound, etc.), but more generally, all forms of the holomovement merge and are inseparable. Thus, in its totality, the holomovement is not limited in any specifiable way at all. It is not required to conform to any particular order, or to be bounded by any particular measure. Thus, the holomovement is undefinable and immeasurable. (David Bohm 1981. *Wholeness and the Implicate Order*. London: Routledge & Kegan Paul, p.151).

Around 500 BC, a Greek named Heraclitus became famous as the "flux and fire" philosopher when he said, "All things are flowing."

In the early part of the twentieth century, Albert Einstein proposed that if quantum theory were correct, a change in one particle in a two-part system would instantaneously affect the other particle even if the two were separated. In 1964, a physicist named John Bell came forward with what is now known as Bell's theorem to prove that Einstein's predictions were, in fact, correct. Bell was able to show that two particles, once together and now separate (even if at two ends of the universe) would change simultaneously when a change to either particle occurred.

Years later, in 1982, an incredible experiment took place at the University of Paris. A team led by physicist Alain Aspect discovered that subatomic particles (under certain conditions) could communicate with each other instantaneously despite the distance between them. It makes no difference whether they are two inches or two billion miles apart. The implications of this discovery are astounding, because it shows the interconnectivity of the universe. It forces us to reconsider the idea of a purely objective world and consider that both the physical and spiritual worlds are constantly interacting.

If we (souls) are part of God and God is Infinite, then what is the origin of the soul? Do souls come pulsating out of this Infinite Being? And if they do, why are they not perfect? Why do they need a physical experience? Whether souls come pulsating from the Infinite or are created by the process of nature, the creation from Oneness to many souls still requires our original innocence. Nature is much more than a beautiful landscape for us to look at; it is an incubator for the creation of souls.

Perfect Oneness does not create souls capable of falling from the grace of God and in need of redemption; this idea makes a mockery of Infinite Intelligence. This is pure heresy, but we believe this in our ignorance, which has its home in our original innocence. Reincarnation helps to explain why it appears that some souls have fallen and others have not. All souls have different levels of knowledge, depending on the maturity of the soul.

Advanced spiritual teachers from these higher dimensions are divided on the belief that we all merge within this oneness of God. Always keep in mind that we never lose our identity as unique souls. If indeed we do attain perfection and merge with God, our identity becomes That That Is. This fear of losing our identity is ego based and not spiritually based in love and intelligence.

FINAL THOUGHTS

"The essential self is innocent, and when it tastes its own innocence, [it] knows that it lives forever."
—John Updike

The origin of suffering, the origin of ignorance, and the meaning and purpose of creation are at the very heart of seeing the perfection of an all-knowing and loving God.

I spent several years on one question after discovering that the origin of suffering was ignorance, and that question is this: What is the origin of the ignorance that the Buddha realized was the root cause of our suffering? Religions had no answers to my question, and the Christian beliefs of a fallen human condition were confusing to me even as a child. My thoughts as an adult were that if perfection created humans with imperfections, there had to be a logical reason for this seemingly unknown reality.

To my surprise, the answer to my question was right there in front of me all that time from the revelation that led to a realization that I had had many years earlier on the causal correlation of variation and a lack of knowledge. If there is no lack of knowledge and only perfection, there is only the perfection of God. Our created lack of knowledge as a soul is our original innocence.

Our ability to see innocence when we experience the sin and evil actions of others will tug at the very heart of our human capability and even our soul. What is as crucial as seeing innocence in others, even our enemies, is to see innocence in our own selfishness and our lack of love for others.

Even if we see ignorance as the underlying reality of sin and evil, we are only halfway there in our level of awareness as to the origin of ignorance. The next step in our soul's progression of awareness is to attain knowledge that the origin of that ignorance is innocence. As we have learned in this book, beyond knowledge is realization, and the realization that the origin of ignorance is innocence allows us to see the world anew.

Jesus, even while being tortured to death, stated, "Forgive them, for they know not what they do," and he taught that we are to love our enemies. What better ideal for humanity, that teaches us to love our enemies? Loving our enemies is not a religious statement, but a spiritual truth about a soul's eternal innocence. Imagine a world where the majority did not judge by appearances, but were able to see a soul's innocence rather than seeing the person as guilty and culpable. We as souls are divine beings, not guilty beings.

"Ignorance is the curse of God; knowledge is the wing wherewith we fly to heaven." Shakespeare

With all due respect to William Shakespeare, ignorance is not a curse of God, but a necessity for creation to occur. But Shakespeare got this right: "knowledge is the wing wherewith we fly to heaven." The hardships, struggles, and suffering that we endure in life, can often feel like a curse of God. Suffering in the midst of time, experiences, and karma leads to compassion, and compassion is always on the path to Shakespeare's heaven.

The world continues to be confused by suffering, sin, and evil, but the confusion would become clarity if everyone understood that ignorance, or the lack of knowing beyond knowing its divine reality, is at the root of what we call evil. The world has yet to discover the necessity of this unawareness in order for creation, meaning variation, to exist. There would be no experiencing relationships with others or the expression of Oneness without variation. All variation equals some degree of unawareness. All ignorance equals some degree of suffering, sin, and evil.

Some religious teachers have taught that when the Absolute, meaning God, manifested the many, a beginning soul's original ignorance became a reality. A more valid spiritual teaching would be that when the Absolute manifested (created) the many, the original and eternal innocence of each soul was born. Innocence always precedes ignorance, just as inexperience always precedes a truth realization.

I sincerely hope this book will give the reader the motivation to seek deeper into these mysteries of life. We were not created with perfect awareness to be predestined robots but to be animated and unique expressions of a dynamic, loving, creative, all-knowing God. The process of creating unique souls is very simple to state but very difficult to comprehend. Simply stated, serial experiences, a perfect feedback system called karma, and the perception of time create every soul as a unique expression of God.

Ask yourself the following questions daily as an eternal soul temporarily living in a human body:

Who must take responsibility for my soul lacking perfect awareness?

To whom or to what do I owe my existence, and for what purpose am I here?

What does it mean that my soul is an expression of God?

The answers to these three questions, revealed in this book, will help to make known to each of us our divine reality as souls and will allow us to see here and now that without our created innocence, we cease to exist as unique souls. Our soul has future potential and unlimited possibilities as it unfolds into a greater awareness of its reality that we can only imagine at this time.

The Creator does not create ignorant souls but innocent souls that cannot take personal responsibility for their own creation. Souls do not create themselves. We as souls are expressions; we are not our own creators. We as souls do not have the option or freedom of not expressing our uniqueness.

Maybe it is best to ask what exists between creation and our ignorance. It is our original innocence, which is actually our eternal innocence, because that essence of love and intelligence that exists within us is spirit. Spirit is the one true reality, and spirit is forever blameless and innocent.

It is the necessity of Infinite Oneness to create unique, infinite expressions of its Oneness. Every one-of-a-kind distinctive soul is created with less than perfect intelligence, which is our unawareness, or ignorance. Attaining knowledge of these simple but profound statements forever changes our view of ourselves, others, and God. The belief in a fallen human status belongs in the history books, as it lacks understanding of God's divine and perfect intelligence.

The meaning of our lives is to be unique expressions of Absolute Infinite Awareness that most call God. Likewise, the only way unique expressions (souls) can be created is if they are created in a perfectly imperfect world. These unique personalities are born of a creative unfolding process of almost infinite experiences: from a spark of awareness to divine expressions of Love and Divine Intelligence. Without our imperfections, there would be no us, just Isness, whatever Isness is, because infinite cannot be defined. We can become aware of and even realize the attributes of this Isness of God, however, such as love, intelligence, beauty, harmony, joy, compassion, and creativity.

How can an Absolute Oneness with perfect awareness and with infinite possibilities express this potential? This Oneness of all that is or ever will be would remain static if it did not create. There would be no universe, no galaxies, no solar system, and not even space—just the stillness of Perfect Awareness.

God must create souls that can interrelate with one another on a continuous basis. Every soul has to be unique and therefore out of necessity a unique expression of this Oneness. In the evolution of the consciousness process, souls perceive themselves to be separate from all other souls. This process creates souls that have a perception of self and others, and these eternal selves can interact with one another. This interaction process is the face and expressions of Oneness.

This process of developing a soul that feels and acts as a separate self creates every soul with less than perfect intelligence and is the source of our ignorance. But with time and experiences and the law of karma, every soul transcends its feelings and beliefs of being separate from all others. This creative process develops compassion for self and all others, and each soul finds joy in being an expression of this Isness of the universe that most call God.

The *involution* process from Oneness to many souls explains our innocence. The *evolution*-of-consciousness process not only creates every soul uniquely but also develops every soul to greater awareness of its divine reality (i.e., the greater the awareness of our soul, the greater our ability to see the innocence within each soul). Our authentic self is our innocent self, which is the spirit within.

The soul has an ego identity, just as the human mind has an ego. The ego is that self that does not realize it is an expression of That That Is, and this ego self feels and acts like it has a separate personal mind. This perception of a separate personal mind is natural and even necessary for the creation of unique souls.

We have not fallen away from God; this ego self is a phase of the divine process for creating unique expressions of Infinite Oneness. We may know intellectually that we are an expression of God, but we have yet to realize that we are an aspect of the Absolute. There's a world of difference between our authentic self and our ego self.

Our authentic self is our spirit, forever innocent. Stated another way, the spirit within us is our eternal innocence. Our authentic self would never harm another being, whereas our ego self, which often lives in fear of others, sees itself as separate and therefore might harm others without realizing that to harm others is to harm self. It is the necessity of creation to create beings with an identity of a false or ego self. This journey of the soul from unawareness to greater awareness creates a soul's uniqueness, and this uniqueness is the dynamic aspect of Infinite Oneness.

Now for a hypothetical question: If you had the option to make the following choice, would you choose to remain within the oneness of the infinite Absolute or would you become a unique soul like no other soul ever created?

To become this unique soul, you have to experience the involution process and become an innocent spark of awareness, not knowing good (light) from evil (darkness). Then after this involution process from Oneness to many, the evolution-of-consciousness process begins. This process is the dualistic journey of the soul that includes the dualism of joy/sadness, love/hate, compassion/apathy, suffering/delight, struggle/harmony, and loneliness/cheerfulness.

This dualistic journey of experiences created by our unawareness is a necessity to create the uniqueness of every soul. A soul's unique identity is created by serial experiences that give us time, and then that universal law of cause and effect is activated. It works as a feedback principle that guides each soul to not only a unique identity but to a godlike status.

Would a soul choose not to take the journey and stay within Oneness, or to live as a unique soul? I think most of us would choose to exist even with the knowledge that we will have to experience human suffering, fears, rejections, and loneliness. We would choose to have a unique identity. To have an identity is to have relationships with others, to love and be loved, to learn to love self as a divine being, to experience the majestic universe and life's challenges, to discover the mysteries of life, to witness a child being born and learning about life—the list is almost endless.

Of course, the reality is, as stated earlier, that we do not have the freedom to be or not to be, as it is a necessity of God to create. Likewise, it is the necessity of every soul to express its unique qualities and attributes as dynamic expressions of the immeasurable Infinite.

We don't have that option to choose because we are expressions of God, and as souls, we do not have the free will not to be created. It is the inherent necessity of God (i.e., Cosmic Consciousness, Absolute, Isness, and Oneness) to express its dynamic potential. One only has to look at the pictures from the Hubble telescope to see the ongoing and continuous creative expression of God's divine glory.

Always keep in mind that the best is yet to come as each soul grows in his or her awareness of unconditional love and divine intelligence. Every advanced spiritual teacher's teachings that I have read that exist in these higher dimensions knows from experience the price we humans have to pay for that awareness, but they all state the journey was well worth it. Even Jesus referred to these higher dimensions as mansions, and what is a mansion but a beautiful home?

Imagine what the world would be like if we humans had more knowledge and understanding about these three profound questions about the mysteries of life. We would see that a soul chooses to live a human life to advance in love and intelligence. We would become less attached to our bodies and crave fewer temporal pleasures. Our ego would realize its highest calling, which is to be an expression of God and to advance the soul.

We humans would become less blaming of others and ourselves, because we would see that creation demands innocence. Judging and blaming create untold misery for the masses. Once we experience total acceptance of self, we see that misery can be replaced with love. We must be willing to open our minds to the reality that God's creation is innocent, and every new soul ever created lacks perfect intelligence for a divine reason.

The belief in original sin and an eternal hell would be replaced with knowledge about soul evolution. This knowledge would help us to see the innocence of our being and the eventual revealing of the ignorance of our soul. The origin of our innocence, which we see as ignorance, is our Creator's necessity to express its infinite self. God creates individualized soul identities that perceive themselves as separate from all others until; of course, they evolve to a level of awareness that sees the oneness of all. That journey of all souls from feeling separate from all others to seeing and feeling the oneness of all is one of the greatest joys of life.

I cannot put into mere words the level of ecstasy we feel when we experience telepathic total acceptance and unconditional love. Only in a dream state that many call a visitation did I experience this reality, which is beyond any words or description. As we acquire knowledge and understanding about these mysteries of life, our individual and collective egos realize their highest calling. That higher calling is a unique expression of God's attributes of unconditional love and divine intelligence.

This uppermost calling is when our ego personality helps our soul live out the drama of human life. This drama provides learning opportunities for our eternal soul to acquire intelligence and to draw ever closer to God. The closer we come to God and become a living reflection of God's attributes, the more our consciousness is infused with peace, joy, and bliss. As humans, we have only begun the journey toward the Infinite, and the time will come when we will look back from these higher dimensions and view new souls with compassion and righteous judgment.

Life is not only a soul's journey to greater understanding, but also an expression of the Divine Mind, and we humans are right in the thick of that heavenly journey. The best is yet to come because with each new realization of truth, we see the world and ourselves anew.

Remember always: we are divine beings not guilty beings.

9271016R00110

Made in the USA
San Bernardino, CA
11 March 2014